Paul
RICARD

Paul RICARD

The Story of Provence's Drinks King

ROBERT MURPHY

weldon**owen**

Weldon Owen
1045 Sansome Street, San Francisco, CA 94111
www.weldonowen.com

Text copyright © Éditions Albin Michel, Paris - 2018

Library of Congress Cataloging in Publication data is available.

ISBN: 978-1-68188-446-2

First Printed in 2018
10 9 8 7 6 5 4 3 2 1
2018 2019 2020 2021

Cover design by Marisa Kwek
Design and typesetting by Meghan Hildebrand

Printed in China

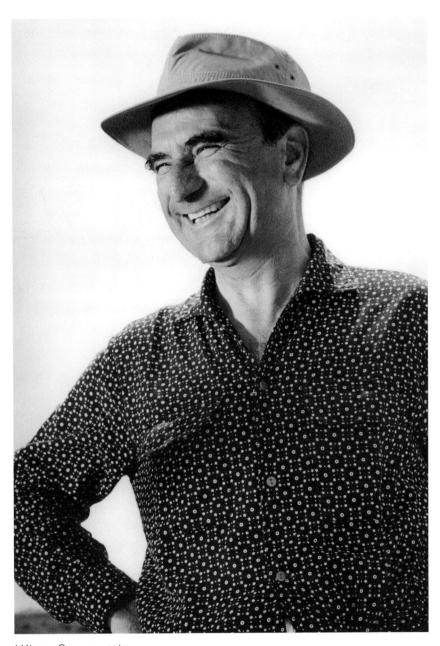

Méjanes, Camargue, 1964.

Prologue

THE ROOM WAS SO CROWDED THAT there was nowhere left to sit. Reporters had crammed into the chateau on the hill above Marseille to hear what Paul Ricard had to say. Rumors had it that the head of the massive drinks empire was going to retire. Some said he wanted to prove a point. That he was going to relinquish the company he had founded three decades earlier to the government to protest high taxes and impossible regulations which, he felt, were killing free enterprise. Others said he was exhausted. In any case, it seemed unthinkable that one of France's most successful self-made men was on the cusp of throwing in the towel.

At 59, Ricard hardly looked feeble. With his strong brow, slicked-back hair, Roman nose, and Cheshire cat–like smile, his bearing was one of an astute field general who knew exactly where to position troops to force capitulation from the enemy without bloodshed. His frame was trim and nimble. He dressed conservatively and neatly, and he brimmed with the confidence of a man who over the years had turned every venture he had put his mind—and mettle—to into gold. Why should a man with accolades, prestige, and millions to his name stop in mid-stride? Why should the king abdicate his throne?

Ricard had made more money than he knew how to spend. His tastes were mostly modest. Pecuniary prosperity was not his aim. Ricard had made his mark by working harder than anyone else. Determination had turned a company he founded in his garage into one of France's industrial jewels. Confidence had pushed him to turn his version of a local anise-based pastis aperitif into a national legend. Ricard brand pastis employed hundreds of people and sold millions of bottles a year.

Most remarkable was that Ricard had achieved his success amid the most historically tumultuous times of the twentieth century. When he started out in the 1930s, financial turmoil consumed the world, reeling from the Great Depression. Later, as the company continued to build steam and experience rapid growth, the Second World War forced him to close.

Never to be beaten, Ricard turned his attention to farming during the hostile Nazi occupation, a venture at which he was equally successful. With the onset of peace, he started his drinks company anew, taking it to even greater heights of achievement.

A man who had staved off so much adversity could not be crushed.

His son Patrick paced back and forth under the hot Mediterranean sun outside the chateau as reporters waited impatiently for his father to arrive at the news conference. "He's not going to do it," he kept muttering to himself. "He can't do it. He just can't."

Paul was stubborn. Once he set his mind to something he carried it out. As leader of his company he had learned that one must make one's own decisions.

Now was certainly the time to show resolve. If he was to retire from the company he had founded, he must make a good show of it. There could be no wavering.

A hush came over the audience at Paul's arrival. He had that effect. People always pay attention to leaders.

His speech started calmly. Paul explained how the purpose of his work had always been to create. Creation had influenced him from the beginning. It had driven his every effort. But as he continued to outline what he saw as the innumerable barriers to his determination, the tension in his voice became apparent. Ricard could no longer stomach the endless roadblocks thrown at him by the administration. He had had enough. It was time to quit. The energy to fight no longer *pumped* through his veins. He needed to let someone else seize the reins and guide the company he loved as only its founder could into a new world. France was in a catastrophic state because of its government.

The media was flabbergasted. Few if any of France's chief industrial actors had come out so resolutely against the government and its policies. As soon as the conference had ended, they rushed to disseminate the information. The headlines of the papers would hardly soften his words.

Le Monde, France's most circulated daily newspaper, said "the king of pastis" was leaving in "protest." *Le Figaro* read: "No chief executive can continue to work under current conditions." *La Marseillaise* said the decision was made "to protest government policy."

"I can no longer stomach the constraints," he told a radio interviewer hours after the news conference. "They are the constraints of an outdated technocratic system that won't admit to change. The system is so outdated that it is no longer capable of driving the chariot of the state. On the contrary, it is a system built to constrain industries like mine."

Paul's message was loud and clear. But did he really need to retire to prove a point? How could a man who had worked to overturn all of the constraints life had *thrown at him* finally have had enough? Where was the fighting spirit that had defined his every venture?

In the weeks following his decision, Paul retreated into himself. He grew ill. A doctor instructed him to move to the mountains for fresh air. Paul stripped away all of the trappings of his hard-earned achievements and moved into an isolated stone shepherd's cottage with only the barest necessities. There wasn't even a phone. Paul had pared his life back to the bare minimum. He decided that he would make cheese and begin painting. The latter had been a passion since his youth. Now he would finally have time to do the things he had been forced to lay aside. The noise had receded. He could be alone.

Men like Paul are not meant for such destinies. Battling the notion of inaction would lead him to a new horizon.

It wasn't long before Paul would be up to his old tricks.

Paris 1956.

Chapter One

WHEN THE EARTHQUAKE HIT ON June 11, 1909, Rose Ricard, who was pregnant with her first child, thought she was going into labor. She was writing a letter at the kitchen table and everything began to shake. Her hand slid across the paper into an involuntary scribble. She was perplexed. Her baby was not due for at least another month. Already he was pushing? It didn't make sense. It was her first baby. Perhaps nature was playing tricks on her mind. Her instincts told her it didn't feel right. She turned to her husband and told him to stop moving the table.

Then, to her horror, she realized it wasn't her husband—or the baby. The earth *was* shaking. Plates and glasses before her clattered eerily as if handled by angry ghosts. Some crashed in a horrible cacophony onto the floor. She couldn't stand up. She fell to her knees. She protectively cradled her pregnant belly.

Rose was experiencing the most powerful earthquake to rock southern France in modern history. It came in rumbling waves. Outside, she could hear people screaming in fear. Across the city buildings crumbled and street pavements cracked. The thunderous sound led some to believe it was the end of the world.

Within seconds it had ended.

Rose stood up and took stock. She was relieved. She and her husband were unharmed, albeit not a little nervous and on edge. The house was a mess with broken plates strewn about the floor, but they could be tidied up. She stroked her distended belly and thought the earthquake must be an omen; she and her son were safe. Nothing could hurt him now. She felt lucky.

When the dust finally settled across Marseille, forty-six people had died and hundreds were injured. Electricity and telegraphs remained down for days. Marseille and its environs, where the epicenter was located, were proclaimed a disaster area. Yet, for such a powerful quake, the toll in human life could have been much more severe. People felt as if they had survived God's wrath.

In the south of France, particularly in Marseille, people socialize outdoors. After work they congregate at cafes, crowding the terrace, especially when it is hot, to rehash the day's events. It had been like that for as long as anyone could remember. Marseille didn't change quickly. It was steeped in its traditions because its traditions made sense. It felt right to be friendly and gregarious under the blue skies, warmth, and abundant sunlight. People in Marseille wouldn't have it any other way.

The summer of 1909 had been brutally hot with temperatures soaring into the 100s. The heat fell like a curtain at the end of the day. Your shirt stuck to your body under your jacket. Outdoor cafes provided an escape from the heat. There was no air-conditioning in Marseille. Indoors was unbearable. In the evening, a breeze would blow up from the glistening Mediterranean. People stayed outdoors even longer than usual.

When the earthquake hit at sunset, most people were still socializing outside. It was a stroke of good fortune. Outside they were safe. The Provencal way of life had served them well.

Rose Ricard gave birth to her first son, Paul, on July 9, 1909, a month after the quake.

Later in life, Paul liked to say that the earthquake defined him. He believed that nothing came without an explanation. When confronted with an event he always tried to shape it, not to let it shape him. Circumstances beyond one's control underscored the balance of the universe. The earthquake after which he was born was a clarion.

Was it responsible for his need for perpetual movement? Even as a child he never let his attention be tethered to one activity. Had it accelerated his capacity to work? To continually produce remarkable results? He was obsessed with creating all his life. He didn't like to sleep. Or was the earthquake merely the basis for his fiery will to live?

Paul was convinced that something that day had shaken his embryonic spirit to its core.

All of the above traits defined Paul over his fruitful 88 years. They made him into a local—and later national—legend, a drinks tycoon who never forgot that Provence had molded him with its sun, warmth, and people.

He was the quintessential entrepreneur who, throughout life, didn't forget his roots. The sun and warm air of Marseille coursed through his blood. He stayed real and approachable, even as his success soared to stratospheric heights. When someone he knew needed something, he went out of his way to help. Paul liked to talk, to share his ideas.

Pushed by a desire to overachieve, he did just that. He built a legendary company from scratch, a business that would flourish and continue to grow well beyond his days. Construction motivated him. It was a desire that inspired him over his life to build islands, ships, a Formula One racetrack, to serve as local mayor, to paint thousands of pictures, and to turn his attention to the environment and the health of the sea, in particular the coast near his beloved Marseille.

Yet Paul's life could have been other. He could have chosen the quieter destiny of his father, Joseph, who imbued a respect for hard work in his son but whose personality gravitated to stability, not adventure.

Paul's appetite for excitement was present from his earliest age. He relished the most difficult tasks. He embraced challenges. He dreamed of conquering the world of business along the lines of the great industrialists of the early twentieth century such as Henry Ford.

While other children his age were busy playing games, he envisioned himself at the head of a multinational firm that would take him around the world meeting people, accruing experience, and seeing sights.

He wanted people to remember his name. As a child he had read about how French automobile tycoon André Citroën lit his name in lights on the Eiffel Tower. Paul could identify with such assurance and panache.

Overachievement lit his inner fire. He could not imagine himself satisfied with the life his father had carved out for himself.

Joseph Ricard started life as a baker. Before him, his father had been a baker. The Ricards, whose lineage was anchored in rustic stability, believed in practicality, hard work, and tradition.

Not that Paul did not value the lessons gleaned from this tradition. On the contrary, he would never forget the lessons he learned in his youth.

The people of Provence were attached to the earth. They respected its cycles and tilled its soil. They knew how to extract the best from nature by listening to it and molding it. Joseph harbored a deep respect for manual labor. It gave him a strong work ethic. It helped him interact with people. Even late in life Paul, who believed that man was made to create with his hands as much as he was fashioned to work with his mind, would spend hours in the woodworking atelier he installed in his home at the Tête de l'Évêque, at Signes, in the rugged hills above Bandol, where he carefully and meticulously carved model boats. If he wasn't carving boats, he was riding a stationary bike to keep fit or sunbathing on his rooftop terrace to soak up vitamin D to improve his health. His life was rooted in industry. He could not suffer idleness.

Paul honored hard work and indeed built the ethos of his success on believing that man improved the world through work. He had seen how toil shaped men, whether field hands laboring under the beating Mediterranean sun, or women, who would walk miles to wash the family laundry.

Unlike his father, though, Paul dreamt of being a catalyst for change. He was a man of the twentieth century. He was no longer tethered to his destiny. He was here create himself.

He believed in the usefulness of tradition. But he didn't consider it static. He had been born into a world in flux, one that would introduce to mankind some of the twentieth century's most important *technological* inventions and improve the life of the masses in unheralded ways.

In the early twentieth century, Paul's native village of Sainte-Marthe, the hillside town above Marseille where he was born, was essentially agricultural. The industrial revolution had been slower coming to the south of France than elsewhere in Europe. Fields surrounded by small Provencal chateaux gave the town a patina of peace and immutability. Wild lilac dotted the white stone-flecked mountains. Men led cows down the unpaved streets, kicking up a cloudy trail of dust behind. The bells on the cows' necks were the background noise of a bucolic symphony. Provence at the beginning of the twentieth century differed little from Provence a century earlier.

Marseille, only three miles away, seemed an incredible distance, the opposite of the quiet, rustic life in Sainte-Marthe. It was a bustling metropolis, a port town whose biggest industry was soap production. *Savon de Marseille* was famous around the world. At the beginning of the twentieth century almost a quarter of the city's population of 490,000 earned its livelihood in the soap trade. Most soap was made in family-operated workshops before being consolidated and loaded onto ships and delivered around the world. Marseille made a perfect location for distribution, and languages from Russian to Chinese could be heard on the dock as boats loaded and unloaded goods that had traveled halfway around the world.

When men weren't working, they gathered outside to talk and play cards. The observance of the ritual aperitif was religion in Marseille. As men sat, time dragged on in such a way that it felt suspended in midcourse. Conversations meandered into the late hours of the night as the heat of the day turned deliciously cool thanks to the breeze off the sea. One almost thought that the sun hung longer in the sky at midday and dusk over Marseille, as if in deference to the conversations unfurling below.

Even the town's geographical location made it special. It was surrounded on all sides by the picturesque hills of Cassis, the rugged Garlaban mountains and, farther off, the Sainte-Victoire mountain, famously painted by Paul Cezanne, who made the mountain into one of the most potent emblems of modernism in art. His cubist masterpieces, in which perspective was deconstructed to reflect the passage of time and light on his subject, was an apt metaphor for the bustling, ever-altering life at turn-of-the-century Marseille.

Every hour bells from the church clanged. Many of the townspeople spoke Provençal, a regional patois mixing Italian and French that traces its origins back to when the Roman Empire dominated most of southern France. Even the horses seemed only to respond to the local dialect as they were driven about on their numerous deliveries.

In 1909, the first electric tramway was inaugurated in Sainte-Marthe. For people in the village the change was immense. Added mobility opened the doors to more freedom. The meandering walk from Sainte-Marthe into town no longer felt so monumental. People moved faster and were able to achieve more in their day.

Paul considered the coming of the tramway the second event to determine the direction of his life. He saw the timeline of his existence underlined by progress. Improvement, he believed, was always possible. It was the essence of his personality, a deep-seated drive to make his environment better, more efficient, and, he hoped, himself famous in the process.

Paul's father Joseph was a freer spirit than his grandfather. As a young man he showed artistic promise and was particularly attracted to music. His ability with the clarinet was good enough to get him a job in an orchestra. He even toyed with the idea that he could make it a career. But it was a short-lived fantasy.

Practicality won out with Joseph. His father had taught him to respect tradition. Joseph realized that a life of music making might be fun but it certainly was not the best way to achieve stability or to nourish a family. He followed his father into the baker's trade. They worked together in Gemenos, about sixteen miles east of Marseille, a small town of 1,000, founded in the Middle Ages and known for its freshwater fountains.

It was a strenuous life. Bread making is physically taxing. Bread must be fresh for the first early clients. Joseph Ricard and his father woke up in the darkness of the early morning, stumbled out of bed, and trudged to the bakery. Work felt never-ending. Little time was left for family or fun.

When Joseph married Rose, whom everyone called Josephine, he had begun to wonder if there might be an alternative to this harsh life.

Josephine was the daughter of a railroad worker. She was born in Marseille, on the *rue des Enfants-Abandonnés*—the street of abandoned children.

As a child Paul felt sorry for his mother, whom he adored all his life. He was certain her childhood had been miserable. It was only logical, having been born on a street with such a terrible name. Paul was determined to relieve the suffering his mother had felt as a child by showering her with love.

In reality, Josephine lived a relatively carefree life as a young girl. Her parents' work brought with it a stable living. Her grandmother told her stories of the French revolution and Napoleon III, whom she had gone to hear speak in Marseille.

Rose and Joseph had known each other since childhood. As children, the two future partners played in the street. They saw each other on the way home from school. In the small circles of their world, they were destined for each other. In many ways, it was a storybook romance.

They married in 1907.

And Rose wanted children.

Joseph had already contemplated changing careers. If he were to have a family, he wanted them to be well provided for and prosperous. Bread making had its limitations. He thought about joining the family wine-selling business that was run by Rose's Uncle Rambaud, a colorful raconteur who liked to brag about showdowns with Sicilian and Sardinian bandits.

When Rambaud died, Rose's aunt, who had no children, decided to endow Rose, whom she adored, and Joseph with the money needed to go into the wine business on their own and continue her husband's legacy.

It was the opportunity Joseph had longed for, the door open to the life he craved. Greater possibilities opened before him. The couple moved to the nearby town of Sainte-Marthe and opened a shop on Rue Moulet.

When Paul was born, he was baptized in the family cellars. The symbolism stayed with him all of his life.

Sainte-Marthe, with its views across the glistening Mediterranean coast, felt to the young Paul Ricard the center of the world. The town was bucolic, surrounded by fields and dissected by small dirt roads. Paul was particularly attracted to nature. He spent hours chasing butterflies. Capturing grasshoppers was another of his favorite games. In the afternoon, he would stretch out in a grassy field and watch the wind blow the leaves of trees. He liked to dream. The skies were an endless blue and in the evening he watched the sunset in abundant colors over the sea.

Paul rose early. Every morning he watched men, who had risen at two or three in the morning, haul vegetables to the central market on horse-drawn carriages. He loved the sound of the horse's hooves clicking on the pavement stones. It was the music of Provence.

His father owned a horse, which was a sign of prosperity because you needed a stable in order to keep a horse. Paul liked riding and was particularly fond of taking the horse on the weekend to Roquefavour, the village where his grandfather lived, about 20 miles from Sainte-

Marthe. Paul knew he was close to arriving at his grandfather's when he spied the soaring aqueduct of Roquefavour emerging on the horizon like a majestic sentinel.

Sometimes Paul went by train to meet his grandfather, who would fetch him at the station with his horse Bijoux.

Later in life, Paul would say: "I think I owe my love of nature to the rural character of Sainte-Marthe. Furthermore, it imbued me with a need to live in a friendly community full of solidarity."

The local *club de belote* typified this idea of community.

Belote is a typically Provencal pastime. It entails throwing heavy steel balls at a smaller ball target. Aficionados trace the game back to the Middle Ages in Gaul, when players tossed stones and later wooden balls.

The game grew in popularity in the late nineteenth century across France. The most ardent players came from Provence where a special variant of the game was developed in which players took a three-step start to throw the ball. The modern game is said to have originated in a celebrated match at La Ciotat in 1907, when a champion, who for medical reasons was unable to take his three-step start, started to play with his feet held firmly together.

His innovation took root quickly, and the game of pétanque was born from the fact that it was now played with the "pied-tanqué," or feet held firmly together.

There were two *belote* clubs in Saint-Marthe: the *Philarmonique,* which belonged to the conservatives, and the *Choral,* which leaned left. Provencal clubs, or *cercles,* as they are known, traditionally split along political party lines.

Heated discussions always ended in amicable partings at the *cercle*. The magic of a drink and throwing the balls at the end of a hot day worked a certain spell that, combined, proved an elixir against animosity.

Founded in 1864, the Cercle in Sainte-Marthe was a pillar of the local community, so much so that it not only served as a gathering spot for men to drink at the end of the day, but also organized dances, concerts, and even lottery evenings. At one point it doubled as a singing school.

Paul liked the Cercle and the men and women who gathered there. Playing pétanque at the end of a sunny afternoon was his idea of how best to blow off steam. It was no wonder that he would associate that pastime to the drink he would create later in life.

Many of Paul's later ideas about life and business were born of the simplicity of his surroundings. It imbued in him a respect for hard work and a suspicion of fastidiousness.

Directness was appreciated in Sainte-Marthe. People did not like to waste time with unnecessary formalities. Paul didn't like fancy trappings, even later in life when he could afford them. His value system was focused elsewhere.

Unemployment didn't exist in Sainte-Marthe. Work defined men and women. There was no safety net of unemployment benefits. Able-bodied people worked. Besides fieldwork, many inhabitants of Sainte-Marthe worked in the local sugar refinery or match-making factory. Others worked in the mines.

"I can still hear—in that wonderful Provencal language—the

reflections on life of those peasants, who knew how to predict the weather and tell the time by the sun," Paul liked to say later in life.

In the afternoon Paul wandered outdoors on long, meandering strolls. There was a small stream nearby. He spent hours building dams with stones and branches. The fact that he could change the course of water at will fascinated him. He constructed sandcastles and small boats that he imagined were traveling to faraway lands. Already he was concocting bigger schemes in his head. It would have pleased his younger self to know that later in life he would build his own boats, finance maritime exploration, and even create an island for the use of artists and tourists.

Above all, Paul liked to draw. In the evening after work, Joseph sat with Paul and taught him how to hold a pencil, how to trace lines, and how to work on perspective. Paul, who found it so difficult to concentrate on most things, showed an innate proficiency for drawing. When he started, all of his attention was focused on his pencil.

A next-door neighbor reinforced Paul's love of the arts. This neighbor guarded fields in the day, but in the evening he spent his spare time fashioning models from wood. His dexterous fingers amazed Paul, who watched intently as he painstakingly built miniature puppet theaters. The idea that one could create something from nothing was infinitely complex and joyous to the young boy.

At five, Paul started school.

Paul's first school was the *Ecole des filles*, or the girls' school. Despite its name, it welcomed both boys and girls. It was one of the first secular schools to open in Sainte-Marthe. France was in the midst of sweeping school reform as it moved to separate state and church. The reforms were being enacted hastily. New schools had yet to be built. Paul's school was housed in a former soap factory.

It was shabby and run-down. Paul didn't like it and found it a makeshift excuse for a school. He felt it was the most ugly place in the world. Its immediate prospects of improvement were slim. War had just been declared.

Fortunately Paul's father had dispensation from service due to a problem with his legs. Times were difficult but remaining together as a family relieved the suffering.

A couple of years into the war, Paul moved from the "girls'" school to the "boys'" school, where he felt more at ease and attached to learning. When lessons pleased him, he proved an astute student. His favorite teacher, Monsieur Simian, wore a bowler hat to class. It was in these classes that he first came across the motto that he would adopt as his own: *Nul Bien Sans Peine*—no pain, no gain.

Monsieur Simian had his pupils write it, among other morally instructive sayings, in the notebooks to perfect their cursive. Paul wrote it over and over in a steady, loopy script.

Paul particularly liked reading about history and the achievements of great men from Leonardo da Vinci to Cardinal Richelieu. Toil and effort cemented the achievements of men whose busts lined the hall of fame in Paul's head. Mr. Simian's lessons got Paul thinking. He, too, desired to play a role in the "great human symphony."

On November 11, 1918, a baker burst into his class to tell Mr. Simian that peace had been declared. His teacher fell to his knees to pray. The children rushed out to sound the joyous clanging of church bells. Marseille erupted into spontaneous celebration.

War was not the only hardship Paul experienced in his youth. He grew strangely ill at age nine. The glands over his body swelled to the size of large olives. He was bedridden and given lessons at home. His family was concerned and puzzled by the strange disease for which no doctor could offer a satisfactory explanation. All variety of remedy was tried. Even arsenic. Nothing helped young Paul's condition.

After months of desperation, a friend of Paul's father offered a simpler remedy for the young boy: he should drink ten and a half quarts of cod liver oil over the winter months and spend the summer by the sea, where the iodine and fresh sea air would purify his body.

The family had nothing to lose. Everything else had failed. Paul packed his bags and was on his way with his mother to the nearby town of Sausset-les-Pins, where Paul's father rented a house. It was raining when Paul arrived in a big coat and a colonial hat designed to protect him from the non-existent sun.

"Breathe in the air, Paul," his mother entreated. "Breathe."

Paul was energized by the sea and took off running along the stone-covered beach. It didn't take long before he returned crying to his mother. He had stepped barefoot on a starfish.

Long afternoons digging in the sand pleased Paul no end. He felt at ease outdoors. Despite his fragile health, playing and being active was what made him happy. Every time Paul was outdoors, he saw things he wanted to paint. Paul romanticized the painter's life, trudging around with an easel strapped to his back and setting it up to capture a magical scene. Convalescing allowed Paul extra time to paint.

One day he met the well-known watercolorist Casimir Raymond, who would paint outdoors all day. Paul watched intently as the artist moved his brush nimbly across the paper. Little by little, the landscape before him would materialize under the artist's hand.

When he wasn't transfixed by the painter, Paul enjoyed playing soccer. He was a particularly good goalie. One of his best friends in Sausset was a boy whose father owned the Olympique de Marseille football club.

The seaside did wonders for Paul's health. His body's swelling subsided and he felt strong again. As promised, the sea and salty air had cleansed his body. He returned to Sainte-Marthe with a clean bill of health. This love of the sea would stay with him throughout his life, manifesting itself in his passion for sailing as well as in his involvement in environmental issues. Later he would even establish a foundation to protect and study the shoreline.

In high school, Paul was particularly keen on mathematics. It certainly helped that his professor in the subject was somewhat of an amateur artist who came over to Paul's house in the evening to give him drawing lessons. Paul was interested in learning perspective. He had a very hard time with drawing straight lines, even if he was quite accomplished when he applied himself to copying a subject.

Though Paul was happy with a pencil in his hand, it wasn't always the case at school. He bored easily and was suspicious of lessons learned in school. All the great men he admired had been men of action, self-made men who had fashioned their own destiny. He respected learning. But learning from rote, as he was asked to do at school, felt to him a waste of time. Action appeared the best path to fame.

He played hooky from school to visit the Longchamp museum in Marseille. Here he would sit for hours, studying and admiring paintings dating back to the Renaissance. Paul loved the masters. They had unlocked all the secrets of perspective and immortalized the moment with poetry and invention. He assiduously labored over his sketchbook trying to emulate their perfection.

The building itself was an inspiration to Paul. Beautiful edifices lifted his soul. The Palais Longchamp was so ornate that it took thirty years to build in the nineteenth century.

Its elaborate beauxarts style, with a sculpted sandstone façade, was dedicated to the glorification of art and science. Besides being a beautiful art museum, it housed a natural science museum and an observatory with what was, at the time, the world's biggest glass-and-mirror telescope. To Paul, science and art together represented the pinnacle of man's achievement.

Paul would boast to his children, and later his grandchildren, that skipping school to visit the museum had been one of the best educational experiences of his life. He wanted them to know that he had been naughty, but in his own productive way. He was never repentant. He wanted his offspring to always challenge the status quo. Breaking the rules for Paul did not go without its fair share of responsibility and work. One must have a rhyme and reason for going against the grain, and once that path was chosen, Paul believed it entailed total commitment.

"The courses I had in high school were outdated, ridiculous, grotesque," he said later in life.

"I learned a lot more admiring the masterpieces at the museum or contemplating the port in Marseille, which, at that time, was particularly beautiful. Men moving baskets of oranges, sacks of salt and cement and barrels of rum."

Despite his son's obvious attraction to art, his father disapproved ardently of Paul becoming a full-blown artist. It should remain a hobby, a viewpoint he made abundantly clear to his son. One didn't make a respectable living as an artist. It was too bohemian a lifestyle, riddled with financial insecurity.

To help his son, Joseph recruited priests to administer lessons to Paul in the evening. Paul liked algebra, geometry, and logic, in which he excelled. One-on-one lessons challenged his fast-moving mind and pushed him to grapple with the limits of his learning. Every summer vacation, he took additional lessons in French and math. But Paul's passion for applying those lessons drove him to strike out on his own. One of his favorite pursuits was chemistry and electricity. He visited stores that made radios to understand the mechanics of how the transmitters captured and transmitted sound waves.

Paul's mother didn't think her son's diffuse attention span would serve him well. He would do better concentrating on one subject and learning it in its entirety. "My mother told me I would never do anything good," he said. Paul was stubborn enough to respect her words but not to follow them explicitly.

He was confident enough in his abilities to know that he would make anything he decided to put his mind to a winning venture. Paul was fascinated by the idea of progress, and he felt that it was in pushing things forward that he would focus his greatest energy.

His father opened the door. Joseph allowed Paul to begin helping with the wine business during his time off and on holidays.

In the morning he took the train on his far-ranging loop to visit bars and cafés, noting orders for clients. He started in Saint-Loup, went on to La Bourdonnière, and then on to the picturesque quarter of L'Estaque, which he especially appreciated. L'Estaque, known as a village of fisherman and tile makers, was a favorite haven for painters. Paul Cézanne had painted it in the late nineteenth century, followed by the likes of Georges Braque, André Derain, and Raoul Dufy. Auguste Renoir loved painting L'Estaque so much that he called its landscape the most beautiful in the world. It was normal that Paul would gravitate to a village steeped in such wonderful history and ambience.

On his way home by the tramway, the landscape to Sainte-Marthe was green, punctuated with fruit trees. Paul was always astonished by the silence of his village once the tram rumbled away. There were no cars, only horses, their hooves clicking on the pavement.

Chapter Two

NICOLAS RAN THE MOST POPULAR CAFÉ in Marseille. The terrace wound onto the sidewalk and people arrived early for lunch. It was hot by noon when Nicolas opened the parasols and people sat in the shade and ordered an aperitif. Nicolas served his drinks with anchovies and olives. It was an extra draw that appealed to his clients. But the major attraction was what he served in the glass. His most popular cocktail was illicit, which made it even more appealing. It was called pastis.

People drank it diluted with water in a glass packed with ice. It had a delicious anise flavor. Though clear when poured into a glass, by adding water it became cloudy. It was like a magical elixir, which was appropriate because it purported to have unusual properties when ingested. As soon as people started drinking it conversation flowed. Men gesticulated with their arms. They told colorful stories that wound on and on. Not only did people feel good after having the drink, but also the drink didn't make them feel bad later. It even helped them improve their digestion.

The café was the favorite stop on young Paul's delivery run for his father. The table talk and the colorful locals carried on all day. He watched enthralled, never bored, as he tried to interpret their conversations. It was poetry in motion, observing the men and women interact. Most discussions devolved into heated political debate. Bistros played an important role in local politics in Marseille. It was as if they had replaced the Roman Forum and the Greek Agora. Many cafés flew the colors of their favorite political candidate during the local election season. Rather than divide people, the heated rhetoric brought people together as they shared their views, despite differences. In typical Provençal manner, most parted with a handshake, friends.

This conviviality struck the keenly observant Paul. Friendship was shared over a drink. The aperitif was akin to religion in Marseille. He started to think he could capitalize on the social mores by harnessing this custom and hitching it to a drink of his own.

"Such demand really hit me," said Paul later in life. "I asked seriously if it wouldn't be interesting to create a product that could satisfy everyone's taste to unite the entirety of the market—a market which didn't even need to be created, because it already existed."

Paul knew the market well. He had spent endless hours in the bars, chatting with owners and customers. He watched carefully how people took their drinks and which were their favorites. He thought long about if and how those drinks could be improved. He believed that knowing his client's desires, aspirations, and needs would prove vital in business. How would a big brand position itself to speak directly to consumers?

He loved to observe people's habits. Once he understood them, he could use them to his advantage. He could play off people's desires and give them what they wanted. Fulfilling desire was easy when that desire already existed. All he needed to do was formulate the right product.

He had wanted to create a pastis for as long as he could remember. The idea had germinated in his mind from childhood. In the evening, after completing a day of work delivering wine for his father, he would repair to a laboratory in his room. He had erected a complete makeshift distillery, replete with barrels in which to macerate herbs and extract liquor. Paul was obsessed. Nothing else mattered. His process started with the distillation of wine to extract the alcohol he needed. Then he added a blend of herbs, fennel grains, and anise. Once it had macerated, he cut it with pure water. He spent long hours trying to get the drink to turn cloudy once it was mixed with water. It wasn't an easy task, and it proved long in nature and completely trial and error in its method. His experiments in chemistry in high school came to his aid. Mixing elements was much like mixing a drink. You needed to dose correctly in order to obtain the desired result. With

Makeshift distillery and laboratory 1930s (left). Paul Ricard at 18.

every try he got closer to what he thought would be a drink that he could make famous across Marseille and Provence.

Pastis was Marseille's prototypical drink. What he wanted to do was to distill that drink into the essence of Provence in his customer's mind. Paul's ideas were clear. The road to perfecting that drink proved long.

One evening Paul worked late into the night. He thought he was getting closer to mastering his alcoholic concoction. With the determination that he showed all through his life once he had set his mind to a task, he continued despite fatigue. He rubbed his eyes and stretched. He thought about taking a break. Then, just as he yawned, his homemade distillery exploded, shaking him awake. It was a small blast, but it quickly started to burn. Paul clambered for the water he always kept nearby in case of an accident. Luckily, he extinguished the fire before any serious damage occurred.

The next morning, when he came down for breakfast, his parents noticed he had burned hair and singed eyebrows. Paul never hesitated to tell a small white lie in the service of achieving his goals. He told his parents it had happened as he was heating his bath. Their house did not have hot running water. His mother appeared to believe his far-fetched story. His father was less credulous. He knew his son's vivid imagination too well. Joseph knew that it was no use scolding his son. Paul had an iron will and would continue in his quest no matter what he said. Already his son had persisted in his pursuit of art, despite his vocal misgivings. Why wouldn't he do the same in his pursuit of making a perfect drink? Perhaps silence was the best way to dissuade him.

Paul's fascination with pastis came from his father. It dated to a meeting with a local legend: a man known as Espanet. He was a former hairdresser who had retreated hermit-like to the Provencal hills to live in communion with nature. Espanet wanted to retreat from society to find the essential in life. He was a French Henry David Thoreau, the transcendentalist who had returned to nature by living out of a cabin on Walden Pond in Concord, Massachusetts. But whereas Thoreau turned his attention to philosophy, Espanet concentrated on hunting and, more importantly, making wine.

Hunters from across Provence knew of Espanet and his drinks. For them, the old man with a long white beard was somewhat of a local sorcerer and curiosity. He gathered herbs and mushrooms in the craggy hills and stockpiled them for use in his alcoholic concoctions. He espoused the beneficial properties of plants. They could heal almost any ailment if administered properly, he claimed. His stone house, or *bastide*, was perched on a hill between olive and pine trees. Nearby, he had a well that was reputed to have the best water in the whole of Provence.

Like most people of the time, however, Espanet didn't drink pure water. It was not thought to be good for your health. The fear of cholera and other epidemics bred through unhygienic water still weighed on the collective conscience.

The ravages of cholera had been brutal during the nineteenth century. During one two-week period in Paris in 1832, for instance, more than 7,000 people died from the disease. Once it ran rampant, nothing seemed to be able to quell its deadly bacteria from spreading.

Espanet's most famous alcohol was one that he would dilute in water. Alcohol killed any disease and Espanet's drinks became renowned locally for their secret medicinal qualities, especially their ability to help digestion. They were also delicious. There was something about his pastis that made it unique. Some thought it was the quantity of fennel seeds he used. Many people tried to pry his recipe from him. But he kept it a well-guarded secret.

In the early twentieth century, wine consumption (and by extension, pastis) did not have the same connotations as it does today. It was drunk at meals in lieu of water. And its consumption was not limited strictly to adults. Often the wine was cut with water, especially in Provence. Many believed wine was healthy— in small doses— for young children. It prepared their palate. It kept them from drinking water.

Joseph Ricard and Espanet were friends. They knew each other as colleagues due to their shared passion for alcoholic concoctions. Espanet had a folkloric reputation. It certainly was bolstered by the fact that he was everyone's instant friend with his easy bonhomie. He never turned away visitors. In fact, he was overjoyed to ply them with his famous drink and to recount tales of his forays into the hills and his ability to find herbs in the most unlikely of places. He liked to watch their faces as they tried his drinks. He wanted to see their true reaction. That was one of his biggest pleasures in life.

As his business prospered, Joseph Ricard bought a car. It was a mark of his success and the solid nature of his business. On weekends, he piled his family into the automobile for a scenic drive through the *arrière-pays,* or backcountry, of Provence.

The car putted along. Twenty miles an hour felt like Formula One racing at the time. It was not uncommon to have to change a tire or tighten an unruly engine belt along the way. If you were a driver, you had to be a makeshift mechanic. Sometimes when the car hit a rock and a tire went flat, Joseph would ask Paul and his brother Pierre to help put on the spare. They would roll up their sleeves in the hot Provençal sun and remove the flat and replace it. By the time they finished they were sweaty and ready for refreshment.

For Paul, the speed was exhilarating. He felt the world whizzing by. He loved watching the Provencal hills approach and then recede in the distance. He loved everything about the landscape: the heat and the fragrant flowers that grew wild in the fields. The ochre-colored earth marked by white stones, wild lilac, and rosemary sprigs. He liked racing past horse-drawn carriages. As they passed a horse he made a point of turning back to wave while he watched the carriage disappear into the distance behind. It made him feel he was advancing at break-neck speed. He felt like he was a clarion for progress. For a young boy who did not like to sit still, it was a sensation he relished.

One hot day, Joseph turned his car from the road onto a small dirt path. The dust flew up behind the car. In the distance, Paul could make out a primitive stone house. It was a stout structure as were many typical Provençal homes. Paul thought it looked solid, as if it had always existed. As they approached, a man with a long white beard appeared. He was hobbling a bit yet also floating. Paul felt like he was seeing an oracle who would predict his future.

The man was Espanet.

As was his custom, Espanet greeted his visitors gregariously with one of his mysterious bottles. Inside the house, bottles lined the shelves. The bottle he picked to welcome the Ricards was special. It was his best aperitif. He liked Joseph and his family. He wanted them to be impressed. After inviting his guests to a table, he ceremoniously poured a small amount into the glasses and then topped them off with water. Paul marveled as the drink became cloudy with the addition of water. Paul and his brother Pierre tasted the concoction. Espanet didn't have fruit juice for the children. No one asked if he did.

Paul loved the drink. It was exquisite rolling on his palate. The anise had a tangy licorice flavor that excited his tongue. There were traces of fennel. It was like tasting the flavors hidden in the Provençal hills.

His head reeling, the young boy began dancing around. Obviously he felt the liquor invading his blood. His dance resembled a Dionysian pagan ritual. His parents asked Paul what he was doing. It looked like he was jumping in some sort of victory dance. The young boy stopped and proudly proclaimed that one day he, too, would make his own pastis.

His father and mother, not to mention Espanet, exploded in laughter.

What Paul didn't realize yet was that the drink he had fallen in love with was illegal and that it had its antecedents in a cocktail that was vilified across much of Europe: absinthe.

At the end of the nineteenth century, absinthe—a highly alcoholic anise-flavored distilled liquor—was France's most popular drink.

Originally it was developed in the late 1700s from wormwood for the medicinal purpose of facilitating digestion.

In the 1800s it gained favor for other reasons.

The French military found it useful in its campaign to alleviate dangers in uncertain drinking water. When combined with water, absinthe killed bacteria. It was that strong. Yet dysentery from putrid water was a serious concern during maneuvers. At times, the disease had been more nefarious than the enemy.

Dysentery, for example, decimated Napoleon's troops in his campaign against Russia. The hydra-headed threats of dysentery and typhus had killed as many as 150,000 troops. Dysentery even wreaked havoc in America. During the American Civil War, an estimated 80,000 Union troops were killed by it. To banish the nemesis, the French military began to ration soldiers with beer, vermouth and—their favorite—absinthe.

Absinthe quickly gained favor and a reputation among soldiers as the drink of choice. The distillery Pernod Fils, which had started in Switzerland before moving to France, produced over 30,000 liters of the drink a day.

Few were surprised that soldiers brought home a taste for absinthe. Many developed a serious habit. When consumed in large quantities, it was found to have psychotropic qualities. Absinthe contained toxic ketones: thujone and carvone, the former sharing the same molecular shape as the primary psychoactive substance in cannabis. The hallucinations it procured provided a mental escape from the horrors of war. That was the fix many soldiers sought.

Others it drove mad. Too much of it seemed to induce mental illness. People started calling it the green fairy, which was either endearing or chilling, depending on the context.

Unsurprisingly, by the end of the nineteenth century, absinthe likewise gained currency with intellectuals and artists. The Romantics had sought release from reality. The French poet Charles Baudelaire had famously proclaimed: "Life was a hospital in which each sick man wants to change beds" and that "It seems that I will be most comfortable in the place where I am not." Baudelaire's release from this ennui was excess. He sought to retreat "anywhere out of this world."

In the aftermath of the Romantic period, the idea of escape still held currency. Retreating into the confines of the mind was particularly attractive. It also underscored a counterpoint to the staid bourgeoisie lifestyle against which so many renegade artists were opposed. Absinthe was bohemia par excellence.

Vincent Van Gogh famously used it and found it particularly conducive to his mysterious mix of colors and exaggerated forms. Pablo Picasso, Edgar Degas, and Toulouse Lautrec all glorified the cocktail by painting absinthe drinkers. The renegade poets Arthur Rimbaud and Paul Verlaine got drunk on the stuff and then wrote sublime poetry. Émile Zola offered a more realistic picture of the ravages of absinthe in his novel *L'Assommoir*.

Marseille was a hub of alcoholic manufacturing. Among the companies producing absinthe were Durand, Berger, Cusenier, and

Rivoire. Even a deputy to the mayor of Marseille produced a version of the drink. Apart from its rebel image, absinthe was a flourishing trade.

The rise in absinthe coincided with a particularly taxing time for the French wine industry.

In the late nineteenth century, the grapevine parasite phylloxera besieged French grapes, almost wiping the country's wine industry from the map. With wine production beleaguered, absinthe picked up the slack among drinkers. Procuring good wine was a difficult affair. Absinthe was brewed in such a way that even the lesser quality stuff passed snuff, especially since most people drank their absinthe by pouring it over sugar, diminishing its inherent bitterness.

Absinthe had its own ritual. A sugar cube was placed on a flat absinthe spoon, which was balanced on the rim of a glass above a small dose of absinthe. Iced water was then slowly dripped over the sugar cube, which gradually dissolved into the drink, causing the green liquor to turn a milky, opalescent white. The recipe called for three or four parts water to one part absinthe.

Hardcore absinthe drinkers took the rite a step further, exercising the greatest attention to let water drip religiously one single drop at a time over the sugar. Anticipation of the final pleasure increased as each droplet altered the drink's complexion.

As France battled the nefarious disease that seemed to threaten some of its best vineyards with extinction, absinthe rose in popularity.

But when the wine industry grappled back to its feet, defeating the insect by fortifying its vines through grafting them with vines from America, which were resistant to the disease, absinthe emerged as unwanted competition to regaining the dominant market position that wine had lost.

If wine were to regain popularity across the entire French population, absinthe needed to be dealt with. Its image needed to be tarnished, even vilified. Wine producers went on the offensive, looking for methods to discredit the green liquor that many had begun to proclaim France's national drink.

The campaigns worked. Absinthe grew to be reviled as much as it had been loved. Anti-alcoholic factions equated it with the devil for its addictive nature. Absinthe was blamed for driving people mad. In truth, it wasn't the drink itself, but chemicals produced in the distilling of inferior absinthe that caused most of the hallucinations linked to the drink. There was little regulation of absinthe distilleries. Industrial alcohol was often used in its manufacture and then colored artificially with dangerous copper sulfate or antimony trichloride.

Countries soon began banning the drink. First Switzerland outlawed it in 1910. The United States soon followed suit. Just before the outbreak of the First World War, France outlawed it, too. France's prohibition included all anise-based drinks.

On March 16, 1915, France outlawed the manufacture and all sale and distribution of absinthe and similar liquors. The "similar liquors," which included all anise-based drinks, were forbidden in a decree on October 24, 1922. Anise was such a dominant top note of absinthe that it seemed only natural to ban all anise-based drinks.

In order to avoid being labeled illegal, drinks had to adhere to a certain number of criteria. The alcohol level had to remain lower than

40 percent, to have at least 150 grams of sugar per liter and to remain limpid after the addition of 7 parts water. Manufacturers brewed alcohol to meet the requirements. To consumers, they became known as *anis doux*, or soft anise drinks.

Although legal, soft anise drinks were highly taxed, with the state levying 50 percent tax on its sale price. And that wasn't the only drawback.

Consumers simply didn't like them. This was particularly true in Marseille. They were too sweet and didn't have any of the digestive qualities people appreciated in absinthe.

In consequence, more people turned to brewing their own drinks to satisfy their taste for absinthe. These may have loosely resembled the drink, but with a flavor all their own: tangy with heavy hints of licorice.

The Provençal substitute was an *anisée* drink like those popular in Greece and Turkey with fennel, anise grains, licorice, and *eau-de-vie de marc*. It was drunk with water—a lot of water—to dilute it. The diluting of the drink was the origin of its name. Pastis in Provençal means "mixture, troubled, something not totally clear." When someone yelled *"Quel Pastis!"*, "what a pastis", it meant all hell was breaking out.

The habit for absinthe was dying a hard death in France, especially in and around Marseille, where the pre-dinner tradition of the aperitif—or *apéro*— was a deeply engrained tradition.

Most Marseille-style absinthes were macerated with *badiane*—a star anise—and licorice. Bar owners and wine merchants brewed their own versions. Clandestine versions of pastis proliferated. In 1932, it was estimated that 15,000 clandestine bottles of pastis were consumed daily in Marseille, meaning a minimum of 300,000 glasses of the stuff per day. It seemed that the people of Marseille couldn't be told not to drink their anise-based drinks. Barmen hid their bottles of pastis beneath the bar so as not to abuse the tolerance shown by most police, who liked partaking of the drink themselves.

The situation presented several challenges for the authorities. First of all, everyone knew that it was going on. Not only was the state not receiving any tax on these drinks, but it was also facing a public health problem if any of the unregulated liquor led to sickness. The drinks posed a potentially grave public health risk.

It didn't make sense to maintain the situation. Logically minded regional officials took to the cause of legalizing pastis.

For many in Marseille, the government interdiction against their favored drink was simply a question of a misunderstanding between the locals and the national government. Their pastis only had a few grains of anise that, when mixed with water, would procure a milky texture in the liquor.

"They failed to realize that this little aromatic grain of anise, known on the shores of the Mediterranean since the pharaohs was used not only in cooking, in baking, but also as a medicinal plant with indisputable benefits for digestion," recalled Ricard.

Paul's father was aware of his son's disillusionment with school. Joseph had always helped Paul in his endeavors. Even when Paul proclaimed he wanted to be an artist, Joseph had taken his son's desire to heart. He was convinced that art wasn't a way to earn a living. "Art doesn't feed a man," he used to say. But he liked that Paul was so enthusiastic no matter what he decided.

He was convinced that continued studies presented Paul with the best path to future prosperity. In his mind's eye, he saw Paul going to university and learning all the lessons he hadn't been able to. Joseph had gone to work early and, through his own hard drive, achieved a level of comfort. He was a father and he wanted his son to do better than himself. But he saw Paul doing it through conventional means.

Paul thought differently. He thought conventions were for common men and he considered himself uncommon. Besides, he was as headstrong as an ox. Once a thought penetrated his head there was no convincing him otherwise. He wanted to start working. He wanted to found his own company. He refused to take no for an answer (which was why Joseph had allowed Paul to pitch in at the family business during vacations).

Paul was thrilled to accompany his father on delivery runs on the horse-drawn carriage around Marseille. They descended the hill from Sainte-Marthe under the hot sun. Once in Marseille they unloaded boxes and trudged them down into their clients' cellars. The work was strenuous and hard on the back. Sweat beaded on Paul's brow and soaked his shirt. But Paul relished every moment. He felt that he was doing something useful. In the evening he was exhausted. He flung himself across his bed when he reached home to rest his tired body.

Sometimes his father would let Paul drive the horses. Marseille was a bustling city full of tramways and hills. The horses clopped slowly down the street, their hooves clicking against the uneven pavement stones. It was a tricky business that Paul managed well. Having watched men drive horses throughout his youth was of assistance now. He learned a lot through osmosis. He believed that most people didn't look intently enough at the world around them. There was so much to learn if you observed. Before you could do your own thing, you had to learn how to copy others. You needed to learn how to do it better than anyone else.

Most difficult was maneuvering the horses after it had rained. The pavement stones grew slippery. One day the horse could not pull the carriage up the steep incline of the rue Aubagne, one of the main thoroughfares through the city. No matter how hard he drove the horses, their hooves failed to gain traction on the slick stones. Finally they threw down blankets on the street so the horses would no longer slide.

These experiences appeared to Paul much more valuable than what he could ever learn at school. Yet his father declined his son's entreaties to drop out. He urged Paul to consider going to business school. Joseph wanted his son to have the tools needed to succeed. Study and a solid diploma would open up doors for Paul, he thought. He would be able to get a good job or take over his own wine business. Joseph knew his own limitations. Maybe Paul would learn something in school that would help push the business into new territory.

What Joseph did not realize was that his son already possessed the greatest tool for success, a trait that could not be learned. He had an unwavering belief in his own abilities. He was convinced that he would succeed and was unafraid to do what was necessary to do so. Paul had no desire for diplomas. They were merely a piece of paper. Learning was what you did when you worked. For all the respect Paul had for his father, he could not stomach staying in school. He wanted to be a man, to earn a living. He wanted to be famous. He could always learn what he needed by reading on his own. He liked reading, experimenting, and enriching his general culture. He loved libraries.

When he finally convinced his father to allow him to quit school, it felt a major victory. Joseph did it half-heartedly. He expected his son would find work too difficult and return to the arcadia of academia.

How wrong he was. Paul now wasted no more time on his path to fame. He knew he was destined for great things. He was 17.

His father did not make it easy going. He sequestered his son in the back office and forced him to learn the intricacies of accounting. For a young man who craved action, the mundane sphere of numbers certainly would cure him of any illusions of professional life.

It wasn't exactly what Paul had in mind when he drew out in his imagination his road to prosperity and fame. But if he were allowed to leave school, he felt he should listen to his father's entreaties to start from the ground up. No pain, no gain.

Besides, the back office was not so bad. There was Mr. Sensier, a former sea captain who had moved to Provence during World War I. He was a curious character who loved to talk and tell tall tales of his adventures at sea. He regaled Paul with the story of how he lost his left leg just below the knee in a terrible shipwreck. Paul's imagination was electrified by such colorful banter. Paul admired the old man's resolve in the face of adversity; every day Mr. Sensier walked two-and-a-half miles back and forth to work, swinging on his wobbly crutches.

Mr. Sensier proved valuable beyond mere entertainment. He instructed Paul in how to keep good books. Over his life, Mr. Sensier had acquired a facility with organizing numbers and making tallies match. Paul took the lessons to heart and soon was doing the calculating himself with natural facility.

Paul was enjoying his time under Mr. Sensier's tutelage, a fact that both pleased and surprised his father. Paul had a mind for detail. Mr. Sensier was an excellent accountant and Paul absorbed his lessons diligently. But Paul itched for more exciting experiences. He put on a brave face doing the numbers, but in the back of his mind he dreamed of being someplace else. He couldn't wait until he turned 18. Then he would be allowed to drive the delivery truck himself.

Paul had trouble focusing on only one task. He was hungry for new experiences and that led him to dive headfirst into any activity that attracted his attention. His mother used to tell him that if he couldn't focus his energy he would dilute his efforts.

Everything was a means to an end for Paul. Foremost among his goals was creating his own company. He was particularly impatient as his obligatory military service was fast approaching. He knew that for one year he would be unable to do any of the experimenting and research he needed for a new product.

Paul created a branded wine that he christened *Canto-Agasso*. Summoning his artistic talents, he designed the label himself. He sketched a small stone house amid a vineyard under the Provençal sun. Already he had figured that drawing on the imagery of Provence would prove his ticket to success.

But getting underway was harder than Paul anticipated. The market position his wine occupied made it virtually an impossible sell. It fit neither into the premium wine brands or the ordinary table wines. It was stuck uncomfortably in the middle. Despite his efforts, the wine didn't gel with consumers. Bars that had tried a few orders did not renew. It was Paul's first failure. It was a bitter disappointment, but it did not discourage him. Paul refused to capitulate in the face of adversity. Failure was a lesson to be taken to heart. He would try again.

Back at the drawing board, he recognized his wine was not developed properly. The aperitif market was more promising. His visits to bars had taught him that much through observation. This time he bottled a marc that he baptized *Cantagas.* It was a modest success. More important, he was building a reputation with the bistros and clients. They liked Paul and admired his resolve. For his part, Paul saw relatively early on that his Cantagas would never be a jackpot success. He still needed to work if he were to make his fortune.

Paul found solace in the pursuit of his other love: art. After years of listening to his father tell him he would never earn a living as an artist, he finally decided to enroll in art school. He was 21 now and working and able to make his own decisions. Even if his father didn't remunerate his work, he now had a job and had proven that he would work hard to make a living. For the moment, his father lodged him and provided a bit of pocket money. But Paul wanted to prove his mettle—even if only to himself. He felt he still had enough spare time left in the day to perfect his artistic talents.

Attending art school felt to Paul the pinnacle of happiness. His first courses were on the torso. He spent hours and hours drawing, striving to perfect every sinew. Then he moved on to sketching from a live model. Paul figured he needed four years before he would be ready to present his candidacy for the Prix de Rome. His sights were set high. If he didn't reach that goal, it certainly wouldn't be for a lack of hard work. He shared his day between working for his father in the morning and studying art in the afternoon. So passionate was he in his endeavors that often he neglected to eat.

Paul trudged to art school every day for lessons between 1:00 and 3:00 and later between 6:00 and 8:00 p.m. For Paul, painting was linked to his moral grounding in tradition. He hated the idea of trickery in painting or betraying a subject. That wasn't to say that he subscribed only to copying nature. But Paul believed he should be faithful to his subject.

Later in life, he would admire Salvador Dali. "I'm not a surrealist, but I admire Dali," he said. "One understands his pictorial language." Paul may not have understood everything that Dali put into his strange landscapes, but he admired the master's hand and the assurance of his brush. Little did he know he would later meet Dali and even buy one of his works.

About this time, Paul's ideas started to grow clearer. Rumor had it the government would soon repeal its ban on drinks at 45 percent. All of the drinks companies were preparing for the day they would finally be allowed to sell the product that so many of their clients demanded: pastis.

Paul heard all the talk in the cafés and bars as he delivered wine for his father. Legalization of pastis was the big buzz. When Paul told his father that they should prepare for the return of the drink, Joseph was somewhat reticent. Other companies were better positioned to profit from the repeal than Paul, who was only an upstart.

Paul wouldn't hear of it. In the evening, he continued his experiments in his bedroom, assiduously dosing his drink. Surreptitiously, he even began sketching potential labels for the bottle. He was an artist, after all. One was always best served by one's own self. He hadn't told anyone yet, but Paul planned to call his drink Ricard. What better way to communicate its quality than to put his own name on the bottle.

In 1932 he finally felt confident in his recipe. It would be the real pastis from Marseille, served with one volume of Ricard, five volumes

First Ricard logo, 1932.

of water and, finally, lots of ice. He didn't quite know it, but Paul had created the first French long drink. And even the overly optimistic Ricard may have been incredulous to know that some fifty years later his company would sell its billionth bottle.

Pouring pastis in the 1950s.

Chapter Three

PAUL RICARD DID NOT INVENT PASTIS. When the government lifted the ban on anise-based liquor, at least a dozen brands jumped on the occasion. In many ways, they had a significant head start on the young Ricard. Most had produced drinks for years. Adapting to the new law required that they merely add another product to their portfolio. They had in place the machinery and distribution network. Some had even been producing pastis clandestinely, selling it on the sly for years. They presented a formidable opponent. If one wished to enter the fray, pulling together a scheme to take on the major players, it would not be easy.

Salesmen from most of the big brands, from the likes of Verdon to Persan, two of the most popular pastis-like drinks, were on very friendly terms with bar owners. They drank with them. They knew their families. They called each other by the informal *"tu."*

But Ricard had something they did not: bull-like determination and an unwavering faith that his product would be premier on the market. He gambled on what he called *le taste*. His drink was (almost imperceptibly) different from the others. His blend of herbs made his drink less acid and somewhat easier on the palate than the competition. He conceived it to be consumed more heavily diluted with water. It made the drink refreshing. Perfect to assuage the heat. He believed his *Ricard* was the best pastis in France.

Anise-based drinks had been part of Marseille's culture in one way or another for centuries. In fact, anise was deeply rooted in the entire Mediterranean basin. One of the first versions of Genesis, the first book of the Bible, recommends a maceration of anise, cinnamon, and licorice to help fend off cholera and the plague. Egyptologists have found references to anise on papyrus scrolls in treatments for teeth, gums, and even the heart.

Paul wasn't a stranger to the ways of doing business in Marseille. It was an insiders' world with preference going to those who were liked best. Once accepted, you had a chance. Through his father's company he had learned to observe that relationships counted their weight in gold. He, too, would build on the connections he had established with bar owners. He wanted to know what they thought. To know what their customers liked best.

Paul was personable. He liked people and people liked him. While developing his drink, he had spent hours conversing with patrons and bar owners.

He wouldn't have called what he was doing market research then— it was a practice only just emerging in the United States— but that is what it was. Ricard's intuition led him to understand the importance of collecting data, tempering it, and tailoring his product to meet his clients' expectations. He wanted to comprehend his target consumers' tastes. The drink he developed was based entirely on what his future customers liked. Ricard did not want to impose his taste. It was the consumer who decided what was best.

"Aren't the best taste-testers the best future clients?" he reasoned.

He had tested his drink during all stages of its development, not only on friends but also strangers. Carefully, he noted their observations and tinkered with his recipe. When the law banning pastis was lifted, he wanted to be ready. His consuming passion was to create the perfect drink. Secretly, he had been sampling a drink that was 45 percent alcohol, above the 40-percent limit imposed by the law. There was also much less sugar than the amount demanded legally. Paul was careful not to be caught breaking the law. Deep down, he believed—as did many in Marseille—that the law was ill advised and would ultimately be repealed. Still, the law was the law and he didn't want any trouble. His drink could only have the properties he wanted if the alcohol content was higher than what the law allowed.

He had cemented relationships with bar owners through his endeavors to market his short-lived Canto-Agasso wine. It may not have been a success, but it helped him understand the key to opening the door for his future ventures.

It was hardly an auspicious time to create a new company. In 1934, the world was reeling from the fallout of the 1929 stock market crash. Franklin Delano Roosevelt was elected president of the United States in 1933 on the promises of the New Deal to restore confidence in the American market. Economic hardship elsewhere had paved the way for a wave of extremism in politics. In Italy and the USSR, Mussolini and Stalin were consolidating power. In Germany, Hitler, named chancellor on January 30, 1933, took outright power on March 23 the same year.

The Great Depression, which started in the U.S., hit France hard in 1931. The middle classes were particularly affected. Unemployment soared between 1931 and 1934. Succcessive governments were unable to bring any relief and budget deficits grew. The situation in France was so dire that it seemed like the country was operating as revolving door. No one could retain power. None could stave off discontent. Six different governments took power between May 1932 and February 1934.

The country was rife with political scandals. To name a few: the Hanau Affair (Marthe Hanau had used his political clout to sap life savings from the unsuspecting); the Oustric Affair, in which the fraudulent fall of the Oustric bank brought down the government of André Tardieu in 1930; and the famous Stavisky Affair, which prompted riots in 1934 and led the French Left to unite its many disparate parties into a single bloc to fend off what they saw as a credible fascist threat.

It was in this context of great political tumult and economic uncertainty that Paul miraculously created one of the great French success stories of the 1930s.

The young Paul left little to chance. He believed man controlled his destiny through planning and charting the eventualities that each project offered. For him, business was like sailing. One rode the wind. But one had to know how to harness it.

"I never improvised," he said later in life. "When you work, you have ambition. If you are not ambitious, it all amounts to nothing. You need a far-reaching objective in order to obtain it."

From adolescence, Paul had aspired to create his own business. In his estimation, it was the only path that would allow him to satisfy his high goals. He always saw higher than others around him suspected.

"I didn't see any other way but to become a great industrialist. Modestly to buy and sell wine like my father was, without a doubt, a nice way to fulfill one's existence."

"We were humble wine merchants, without a vineyard," rued Paul. "Selling wine would never lead to fame."

Living the life of others was never to be Paul's style. He set his objectives at the highest level.

"I took as my examples Louis Renault and André Citroën. They had started as artisans and built their business into empires with important factories."

Even in his youth Paul envisioned his father buying all of the buildings surrounding the family wine depot. He saw his empire quickly proliferating. Flags flew from the roofs, announcing his important achievement and position.

Nothing he drew in his mind's eye was small. When he was convalescing as a child at Sausset, he dreamed of sailing. Not merely sailing. Commanding an entire fleet that controlled the Mediterranean. Even in his dreams, the Mediterranean wasn't enough. As soon as he decided to rule the Mediterranean, he set his sights on expanding his fleet to sail the waters of the world.

He saw what the locals drank in the bars in Marseille. It was a market driven by aperitifs. All along the café walls were posters of the most successful: Cinzano, Bonal, Saint-Raphaël, Mandarin, and Dubonnet. Why shouldn't he have his own posters? His own brand of drink that people ordered by name?

Paul remarked that none of the most famous drinks were universally popular. The market was fractured. If the government lifted its ban, pastis, he thought, would become the signature drink of Marseille. A drink that everyone would love. It would be the drink of Provence, par excellence.

Everyone he met got to taste his latest tinkering with his pastis. He carried a flask of it around with him wherever he went.

"Tell me what you think," he would entreat both friends and strangers. Each time he went into the bar he would set the flask mysteriously before the owner.

His drink was velvety on the palate, but it still looked a little green in the glass, people told him. Everyone had an opinion—and they were not all favorable. Paul took them all to heart. He modestly heeded all suggestions. He wasn't a connoisseur, not having drunk much liquor before he started on his task. That lack of finesse was to be used to his favor. He didn't let his own tastes get in the way of a drink that would please the largest number.

After a night spent in his laboratory distilling his drink, taking into account the most recent suggestions, he took the modified elixir back into the field for testing. It was as if he was retouching a painting in an attempt to finally turn it into a masterpiece.

When he finally felt that he had distilled the drink to the right proportions, he was ready to put it on the market. First he needed a name. Just as with his drink, everyone had an opinion. On this point, however, Paul was unwavering. The only name it should carry was his own. If he believed in the superior quality of his product enough to put his name on it, then he could do nothing else but succeed.

One night at dinner he dropped the news: "I'm ready to launch my pastis," he said.

His parents looked at him with surprise. They thought Paul was off on one of his habitual monologues about a new project.

When he insisted, they began to take him seriously.

"It will be called Ricard, le vrai pastis de Marseille." "The true pastis of Marseille."

Not everyone in his family was as enthusiastic as Paul when the government lifted the ban on anise-based drinks on April 7, 1932.

His father thought the market for the drinks would obviously grow. In fact, he thought there would be a mad rush into the market. But so many others were better positioned to lead the charge. His son had only limited experience in taking on such hard work. He didn't even have proper distillation equipment. He was working from the hip, improvising as he went along. He was making pastis literally out of the garage.

Paul may have shown a certain nonchalance that worried his father, but Joseph felt Paul's optimism. His son's conviction that he would succeed was unwavering.

It was based on Paul's enthusiasm alone that his father donated 600 liters of alcohol to his nascent project. It would make about

1,200 bottles of Ricard. Paul bought three old absinthe barrels from Pernod and some one-liter bottles. If he could make a go of it with these modest means, perhaps he could convince his father that he was onto something.

The young company was like a family. The back rooms of the family wine business on the Rue Berthelot at Sainte-Marthe were transformed into a makeshift office, stock rooms, and factory. After dinner and often late into the night, friends would help with the filling, labeling and stocking of bottles while during the day Paul and his brother Pierre took care of deliveries, invoices, and orders.

It was intense and not without risks. His father often told Paul that he was leading the family into folly.

"My father was a wine merchant," recalled Paul. "He used to say, 'You are going to ruin me with your pastis.'"

Paul indeed was onto something. As soon as he started delivering bottles the business exploded. He sold 30 bottles the first day, and a week later a bar asked for another 30. Paul could not believe it. He already faced the problem of inventory. He didn't have any. He would have to scramble to have another ten bottles delivered.

Soon, orders were pouring in.

"Your idea for pastis is not such as bad one," Joseph told Paul, who took the words with silent pride. But Joseph remained prudent.

Paul said nothing. He was convinced his father was too conservative. His main priority was to construct a small factory that would allow him to scale the heights of his ambitions. He convinced his father to invest.

Joseph Ricard bought a plot of land next to his wine warehouse, and Paul bought a bottling machine and ordered the construction of large distilling tanks. He hired four office employees to oversee invoices and orders, four others to help with manufacturing, and two men for deliveries. Paul and his father spent all their waking hours beating the pavement in Marseille to drum up business and help promote their nascent brand.

Factory in Sainte Marthe, 1936.

"We worked night and day," he said. "It was a passionate adventure."

He approached every obstacle obstructing his objective as an opportunity to create, to outflank the competition, and to build the empire he desired.

He loved people and chatting. It was part of the local mystique. Small talk and bonhomie were considered integral to a good character.

In Marseille, you could trust the man you could talk to.

Paul's relationship-building skills earned him a reputation among the owners of cafés and bars. He also seemed to have in mind the best interests of his partners.

He wanted to bolster their bottom lines. Unlike so many of the anise-based liquors on the market, Paul's pastis was positioned as a less expensive alternative to be consumed in small doses as it was heavily diluted in water.

A normal bottle of aperitif yielded between fifteen and twenty glasses. A bottle of Ricard yielded 50—even 100 glasses when used sparingly. The bars were happy because consumers would buy several glasses per visit. Profits obviously would be higher.

Paul wanted everyone to have pastis. "*Pastis pour tous,*" was his motto. "Pastis for all."

Ricard instinctively recognized the importance of image. As a would-be artist, he had been impressed by the power of visual representation from his youngest age. Some of his most intense memories in childhood were caught up with art and learning how to draw. Messages were communicated through art, but more importantly it was a lightning rod to harness emotion.

When he visited bars on delivery runs for his father, he had seen the marketing power of posters. Drinks had to tell a story, and the more they could equate their drinks with a distinct storyline the longer they would stay loyal to that drink. The choice of spirits was not merely a matter of taste, although that was primordial. Image had a very important role.

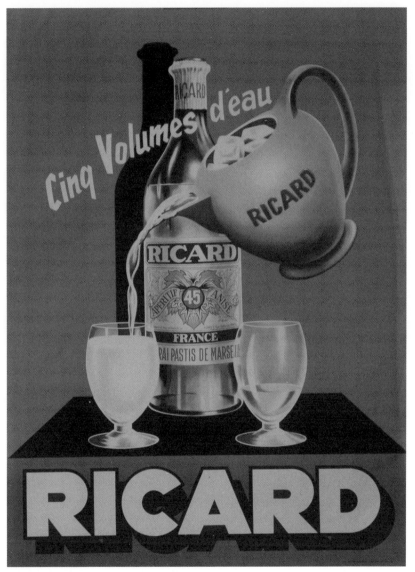

Poster from 1960.

Paul knew the story of his drink by heart, and it had to do with the spirit of Provence, the conviviality of Marseille, the sun and the sea. Now he had to package those ideas into a brand. It would be a long road to convincing people, but Paul's ideas were crystal clear.

His advertising campaigns started modestly. He thought it important to educate his customers in not only the culture of the drink, but also on how it was to be drunk. Many of his posters instructed people how to dose the drink with water and ice.

In 1939, he offered one of his early memorable campaigns. It featured Darcelys, a local singing star from Marseille whose best-known song was called "Une Partie de Pétanque" ("A Game of Petanque").

The association between the singer and Ricard was obvious for Paul. The favorite local game should be linked to what should be the favorite local drink. The posters featured the singer with a *casquette* perched on his head and the singer standing in three-quarters profile, his hand to his mouth as if amplifying his message. The tag line read: "Garçon! Un Ricard "À la Marseillaise"," or "Waiter! A Ricard, Marseille style."

The ad's color scheme reinforced the imagery that Paul wanted to communicate. The poster's blue background was evocative of the sea, while the yellow bubble holding Darcelys' words was the yellow of the sun. The singer himself wore a green suit, which harkened to the color of Paul's drink.

The advertisement was a resounding success. It led to a long association between Ricard and Darcelys. Over time, the singer

Poster featuring Darcelys, 1939.

became one of the most effective spokesmen for the brand. He recorded songs such as "Un Pastis Bien Frais" (A Well-Chilled Pastis) or another simply entitled "C'est le Ricard." The recordings were distributed by Ricard and played in bars to spur demand. Darcelys's music encapsulated everything Ricard wanted to purvey. The songs were upbeat and sunny, full of joyful accordion compositions that one could imagine playing as revelers danced under a full moon on a supremely warm evening. Paul's Ricard was "Le Vainqueur de la Soif," or the "Thirst Quencher."

Marketing alone would not drive Paul's success. He knew that his own people would make or break his pastis, no matter how good the initial idea. It was absolutely necessary that he create a convivial environment for his employees, that they could feel at one with the company as they would with their own family. He knew that Citroën and Renault—two of his idols—had created close links to their employees. It was certainly true for Henry Ford, whose socially advanced work culture Ricard held in the highest esteem. The employees needed to believe as much as the boss did in the viability of Paul's project. For Paul, there was no example of a boss who had succeeded without being competent in his employee relations. The boss needed to be loved and respected.

This would remain one of Paul's pet peeves throughout his life. He believed such a working environment represented the exact opposite of state technocrats who were, according to Ricard, poisoning France. Paul wanted his employees to believe that they too could become the boss eventually if they worked hard enough. They could become affluent. They could own homes. Ricard detested the idea of a power struggle between classes. Free enterprise abolished that if it operated correctly. It had to be close to its people. He believed that the company ultimately positioned itself closer to the people than the elite political class.

When Paul was young, much of this philosophy was born from what he saw and experienced. Poverty was rampant. During the First World War, he saw children who scraped by on charity. This alone helped to motivate Paul to work harder than anyone else. He felt a responsibility to society, to help it improve and move forward. Work was a responsibility that needed to be taken seriously. Improving one's lot involved improving the environment of everyone around.

"The purpose of a great nation should not be to strengthen the powerful or to further enrich the wealthy, but rather to raise the standard of living for all. It is not a question of ending wealth, but of ending poverty," said Paul Ricard.

Often Paul chastised himself. He felt lazy, that he wasn't doing enough. He found himself not good-looking or intelligent.

"That's why I worked more than most people," he said later in life. "I see people that take themselves seriously, people who think they are intelligent, and I see pretension—there is a lot among the French administrative class—people who want to teach you a lesson, who think they know everything and who want to rule on other people's happiness."

More than anything, Paul wanted to build. His ideas about business went hand in hand with those on leadership.

"Every company, like every community, needs a leader. Therein is the reason to be a leader. Leaders are for leading, not for managing, because one must not mistake leading for managing."

"I could have become a politician," he continued. "I decided to be useful, to build the company I founded with my father and to help create a better life for those around me."

Obviously Paul was set to ruffle a lot of feathers. The competition viewed him as a brash upstart. They thought he would burn out and fade away, a shooting star on the drinks landscape. Ricard had other ideas. He may have come out of nowhere to threaten their market share, but he wanted to make sure that he would be on their heels for a long time.

Paul was determined not to let them have an easy ride. In his first year of operations, 1932, for which he only counted eight full months of sales, he sold a whopping 364,000 bottles of pastis.

His father was impressed. He thought that at this rate they could eventually sell 100,000 bottles of pastis a month if they prudently built their production and sales capacity. It would be a great achievement, he told Paul, who only shrugged at his father's prediction.

Paul had set his goals much higher. His immediate goal was to sell as many bottles as his father thought could be sold in a year in one day. He pictured the company selling millions of bottles a month. How could he have told his father that 50 years later the company would be selling 70 million bottles of Ricard a year.

Most laughed at and few believed in Paul's predictions for success.

When he told one sales representative in Nice that he should increase his 1,500 liters of Ricard a month to 5,000, the salesman responded with an incredulous chuckle. He thought 2,000 liters a month was a good goal. Two months later, the same representative was selling 15,000 liters a month to clients in Nice alone.

Paul's enthusiasm was infectious and spread like wildfire.

Ricard worked night and day. More friends, school pals, and even neighborhood children were recruited to pitch in. There was so much work to be done and not enough time to make and deliver enough pastis to fulfill demand. Ricard knew that if he couldn't fill orders, business would suffer. Customers would lose confidence in his ability to provide the product. Paul sometimes worked so hard that he simply forgot to eat or, at times, even sleep.

"At one point I thought if the government could outlaw us for a while it would give us time to get the right equipment in place," said Paul later, referring to the production challenges of the time.

As business grew, Paul had to work out thorny logistics and

card's children in the 1940s (left). Marie-Thérèse and her children in 1960.

atrick and Paul Ricard, at the 45th birthday of the Ricard Society in 1977.

Early advertisement from 1938.

Poster featuring la Caravelle in 1952.

La Caravelle, Tour de France in 1952.

Pitcher design evolution. From left to right and top to bottom: 1952, 1953, 1953, 1954, 1954, 1970.

Ashtrays, 1970.

Carafe design evolution. From left to right: 1934, 1953, 1953, 1958, 1958, 1965.

Ricard bottles from 1932, 1938, and 1953.

Paul Ricard shooting session, the 1950s (left). The VIIth International Festival de Cannes, 1954.

La Maison du Printemps poster, 1950.   *Porte d'Orient* poster, 1950.

La Caraque Blonde posters, 1953.

Advertisement featuring Tilda Thamar, 1955.

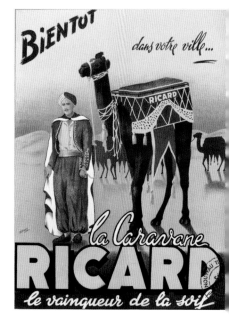

Advertisement for Ricard when the Suez Canal was closed in 1956.

Delivery of bottles via camels when the Suez Canal was closed in 1956.

balance sales with costs. Demand was high across the southern part of France. Delivery in those days was difficult and costly. Even getting bottles to Nice, which was only 125 miles to the east of Marseille, was a challenge. Most of the time bottles were delivered to Nice from Sainte-Marthe via boat.

"It was ten times less expensive than the train and half the price of delivering by road. At that time we paid attention to profits. Even deliveries to Lyon were made by boat. It took a week. But it was significantly less expensive."

"The more I grew the more I knew I had found the secret of success."

Paul kept his target in mind.

He paid his representatives on commission. He also quickly realized that well-paid sales representatives were one of the keys to success. Every surge in growth was awarded a bonus.

Representatives were hired across the country.

Transmitting his faith in the company to his employees was meant as a motivator for Paul. He told his employees that they would profit as much from his success as he.

Paul knew that his success was rooted in personal relations. He also realized that he needed to imbue this work ethic and bonhomie to his sales team. He exhorted them to always wear a tie, even in hot weather, and to make sure their trousers were well pressed with a sharp crease.

Paul wanted to anchor the image of his pastis with that of his city: Marseille. He recognized the power of its dolce vita in the imagination of not only those who lived there, but also, more importantly, those who did not. Sun, sea and pastis with the beautiful imagery of Provence would prove a winning formula.

Paul's exceptional success in such a dour economic and social environment obviously had something to do with his own person. His belief in success drove himself and propelled his employees along with him like a supercharged locomotive leading a long train. He had an innate sense of the market from having observed it from the inside out for so many years thanks to his father.

The decision to position his pastis as a drink for everyone was primordial. His "pastis for all," with a glass of his aperitif appreciably less expensive than others, proved prescient in wrestling market share from his larger competitors. Paul was proud to be a man of the people—something he would maintain all his life—so it was natural that his drink would be for them too.

But beyond his nose for marketing, Paul's company organization and his staunch belief in self-financing all of their projects helped keep the company turning at full speed. No one would be relied on outside of a small family group.

Ricard's parents and his brother Pierre (left). Paul and Pierre Ricard in the 1930s.

The shareholders in the company would be restricted to the family, a small group of investors, and primarily the employees. Getting the most out of employees meant giving them more than they expected at the time. When in the 1930s two weeks of vacation were the norm, he offered his employees three. At the end of the year he awarded them shares in the company, which was totally unheard of at the time. He espoused what he called "popular capitalism." It meant that everyone worked to get rich, but that he would take care of them as it happened. None of the communist ideology that was bubbling up from the intellectual and political classes at the time made sense to him. He thought it dangerous and a road toward social unrest. There was class warfare in Paul's world. He himself had worked his way up from the bottom, and he hoped that his employees would do the same. At least he would try to help them move as far up the social ladder as they could.

When he paid his representatives on commission, they were automatically motivated. At the end of the day they knew exactly how much they had made. Paul believed in the simplest of logic and accounting. When you covered your expenses you should be making money.

The system he put in place was working. Employees were working double time—and making double money. For Paul it was proof that despite the political and economic upheavals of the time, hard work triumphed. You could determine your own reality. You could defy the odds. All you had to do was believe. Believe in yourself and your vision. And then work like a madman.

Chapter Four

PAUL WAS IN A GOOD MOOD when he arrived at the wedding of his friend Paul Cognet in Lyon. It was 1937 and Paul's business was booming. Founded five years earlier, the company had grown from an operation run out of his garage to a full-blown enterprise that employed hundreds of people and had its own factory. In fact, business had been so good that Paul wondered at times if he had enough capacity to fulfill demand. It was a nice problem to have.

As he arrived at the wedding, Paul quickly found Cognet, who worked at one of Ricard's concessions. Paul grabbed his hand firmly. He asked Cognet about his future father-in-law, whom Paul held in the highest esteem. Dr. Louis Thiers was the kind of man whose reputation preceded him. Paul admired anyone who practiced a trade not for money alone but equally for the satisfaction that the work provided. That was particularly true of Thiers. He never turned away the poor and hardly ever asked that they pay for his medical service. He was a man of principle and social awareness. Some considered Thiers a maverick, which Paul admired most. Like Paul, Thiers marched to the beat of his own drum.

Ricard himself felt that he wasn't working merely for money.

Monetary reward, of course, was important. But it was work itself—
"man's duty," he liked to say— in which he found fulfillment. He
felt a responsibility to contribute to the "great concerto" of human
accomplishment. To push the human story forward was motivation
enough. A man must find his calling and adhere to it, building success
brick by brick through diligence and hard work.

Dr. Thiers was a Good Samaritan. Why should only the rich
be entitled to treatment? His paying customers provided him with
enough to allow him to provide free services to people in need. Locally
Dr. Thiers was a folk hero—and he was loved, a fact reflected in the
dozens of turkeys, sausages, and hams he received from his clients
every Christmas in recognition of his aid.

Cognet's marriage was a fantastic party. Food was copious and the
music very satisfying to listen to. Paul did not often go to parties. He
didn't have the time. He had hardly had time to think about anything
related to pleasure over the last five years. Besides, he felt thoroughly
uncomfortable dancing. He would rather watch than participate, and
was most comfortable listening, soaking in the ambience.

He was happy to see that people were drinking his Ricard far
from Marseille—in Lyon no less—and having a really good time.
He felt as if he had brought a little of the Mediterranean sun to the
center of France.

As he listened to the music and talked to friends, an attractive
woman caught his eye. She bore a passing resemblance to Edith Piaf,
with a high forehead and deep, dark eyes. Paul was intrigued. She was
the sister of Paul Cognet's new bride. What good luck. He asked that

they be introduced. She seemed even more beautiful to Paul when they started to speak. Paul was a decisive man. Immediately he knew that he had met his future wife. Her name was Marie-Thérèse.

It was a whirlwind romance. He never hesitated to pursue what he wanted. Paul was excited to share the news with his parents. He had worked so strenuously over the years that romantic attachments found no place in his overly busy schedule. Even as a schoolboy he had hardly found time for girls. Experiments in electricity and chemistry, not to mention his painting, filled his hours. It was complicated to kindle relationships with the opposite sex. Most meetings were clandestine. Otherwise, boys and girls found themselves under heavy supervision. Paul's mother encouraged him constantly to get out and meet girls. She did not want her son to miss out on the joy of family. Paul thought eventually that he would found his own family. Work took so much of his time. Family could wait.

Mrs Paul Ricard by Tafuri, 1950 (left). Wedding portrait of Paul Ricard and Marie-Thérèse Thiers, 1937.

Now, with Marie-Thérèse at his side, he could plot his legacy.

Paul brought home the good news. He was anxious that his parents, especially his mother, share his satisfaction. Rose Ricard was elated. She had dreamed of having grandchildren around her. The sound of children rumbling around a house filled her with joy. Rose believed strongly that family served as the roots to a person's existence.

The courtship was short and Paul and Marie-Thérèse were wed. Paul believed he had just opened the door to a long period of prosperity and happiness. With his company growing and his family happy, Paul felt that he was on top of the world. Little could he suspect that the next decade of his life would prove the most difficult, riddled not only by personal tragedy but also by global strife and struggle.

When Paul's father fell ill no one in the family panicked. It seemed little more than a common cold. When his condition suddenly worsened, the family grew gravely concerned. No one wanted to believe that Joseph was dying. But it became painfully clear quickly enough. Paul's mother instructed him to hurry to Chambéry, some 250 miles north of Marseille, to bring home his brother. Pierre had been working as a company representative in the mountainous Savoy region, near the Italian border. Rose knew that no time could be lost if the two boys were to bid adieu to their father.

Paul set off immediately. Despite their determination and speed, Paul and his brother reached home too late. Joseph Ricard was already dead when the two boys returned to Sainte-Marthe. He was 52.

Paul was devastated. His father had been his moral compass, his companion in business and, above all, his friend. As he stood over his father's deathbed staring at his inert body, memories of his youth flashed through Paul's mind: Days spent traveling through Provence at his father's side, his father explaining to him the lay of the land and which trees had what name. He remembered driving his father's horse-drawn carriage slowly through the labyrinthine stone-cobbled streets of Marseille delivering wine. His father always wanted the best for his eldest son. Joseph recognized the insatiable drive in Paul's character. He did not want to extinguish it. He tried to channel it. He asked Paul not to be distracted, to focus his talent and not spread his ability too thin in his desire to discover and try new endeavors. Joseph never raised his voice with his son. He only had encouraging words for Paul.

Paul felt the heavy weight of responsibility crash down on his shoulders. Now he was alone in his role at the head of the company. An entrepreneur himself, Joseph Ricard had paved the way for his son to start in business. Although Joseph did not show the same certitude as Paul in the beginning due to his prudent nature, he believed Paul had hit upon a wonderful idea with pastis. He was proud to be a part of his son's fantastic creation, which soon became instrumental to the prosperity of the entire family. With his father gone, Paul felt himself swimming against the current in a gigantic pool, alone. His father had helped to raise the sails, but Paul would be left to sail the ship alone.

Paul was 27. He was set to learn a quick lesson in the politics of responsibility. Though he started by seeking counsel from senior employees, he realized soon that he was master of the vessel now. No one could make the decisions for him. He had always had long discussions with his father about each important issue for the company. Paul called it a permanent dialogue. They influenced each other with opinions, using each other as sounding boards to understand and follow the most effective path. He had a counselor and so did his father. When that pillar was gone, Paul's first instinct was to replace it.

"I thought I needed advice," he said later in life. "Well, I asked. I sought direct advice from my managers and representatives. They replied, 'We will follow you blindly.' It was a heavy responsibility!"

Cash was an immediate issue. Demand was so high that the company was whirling at full speed with high-cost production. Although money was sure to come in, investment needed to be made first. Bottles needed to be bought. Raw materials had to be secured. Joseph had been the figure of stability that reassured banks and investors of the company's viability. With his death, many of those relationships froze. Joseph's bank accounts, through which the company was run, were suspended in limbo as the state worked through his succession plans and will. For a company in early expansion mode, turning off the spigot of capital proved a tricky—and seemingly *life-threatening*— situation. If production could not be paid for, how could they sell and how could they continue? Paul worried that if he could not continue to finance the company he would see his dreams die as quickly as they had been realized. If he could not supply his drink, he would lose his market and the faith of his clients.

Before his father's death, the company was a loose organization under the umbrella of Paul's father's businesses. It was run separately but, on a legal front, integrated with the rest of the family holdings. With Joseph's assets frozen, it became imperative for Paul to generate the cash necessary to keep the business flowing and bottles filled. Paul took the initiative to demand payment in cash of all unpaid deliveries. The total sum tallied some 500,000 francs. Armed with a revolver to guard against robbers, Paul took the money to the Banque de France, where he deposited it. Now he could honor payments he was no longer able to make through his father's accounts.

The next order of business was to reorganize the company structure. Paul put his family first, so it was only natural that his mother and brother Pierre be named to the board, along with himself. He needed to appoint seven others to oversee the board. This is where Paul would diverge from his father and prove himself a pioneer in corporate governance and employee benefits. For starters, Paul believed the best way to get productivity from his employees was to have them participate directly in company performance. If they felt vested in the firm, they would, undoubtedly, expend the greatest effort to make it prosper. Although a common idea today, attributing shares to workers was a new concept in the days before World War II.

Paul felt himself a progressive in the realm of worker-company relations. Henry Ford's idea to pay workers enough to buy the products they made (controversial at the time) had been hugely inspiring to him. Paul considered himself a worker and did not feel himself superior in the way many could imagine. He wanted workers to prosper so he could as well. It would be an idea that would guide him throughout his life as the head of Ricard. So as he moved to reorganize the company structure in the wake of his father's death, he decided that employees would be attributed free shares in the new company structure. Likewise, he named seven employees to help oversee the board.

It was a revolutionary move but it soon became usual to give stock options to employees. Paul was introducing socially responsible ideas into his firm not by any philosophical bent but from his sheer common sense. Elsewhere in France, the socialist Front Populaire leftist coalition had assumed power in the government and was instituting wide-ranging reforms in favor of easing workers' difficult lives. Their measures included paid vacation and the reduction of the working week. Strikes had broken out at factories across France and workers were showing their determination to change the status quo. But apart from catering to workers' rights, Paul felt clearly that it was important to treat his employees as part of a family. If he took care of their best interests they would take care of his.

Yet as Paul wrestled with these organizational issues, he suddenly was confronted with another personal tragedy. His younger brother Pierre died after a battle with tuberculosis. For Paul, it was a double whammy. First his role model, now his confidante was gone. Like his father, Pierre had always encouraged Paul in his endeavors. When Paul's father had dismissed Paul's first attempts to make pastis as mere folly and his mother had chastised him for the mess he made at home, Pierre had encouraged his brother wholeheartedly. They conspired together to create a perfect drink.

Pierre's disease devastated his body quickly. Not long before falling ill he was cycling like a champion. Pierre spent almost every

Paul and his brother, Pierre, around 1920.

Sunday participating in local bike races. On one Sunday, however, he passed out cold during the race.

The family dispatched Pierre to Chambéry to convalesce in a sanatorium before resuming his activity in the firm. Meanwhile, Pierre kept his fingers in the family pie by overseeing the Ricard distribution center for the region. Paul made numerous trips to visit his brother and had fond memories of skiing and driving his car on the frozen roads.

Paul was now more alone than ever. In response, he threw himself into work. It was a futile attempt to assuage his suffering. But professionally, Paul's work reaped huge dividends.

The company grew in leaps and bounds. Paul knew that growth was the key to success. "A company is condemned to grow," he said. "It dies otherwise. If there is no evolution, then there is death." Paul believed that everything is movement. "Victor Hugo said even dead trees evolve. Nothing is immobile."

Marseille in the 1930s was riding a wave of popularity helped, in part, by the new medium of cinema. The writer and filmmaker Marcel Pagnol earned acclaim for his films about Provence such as *La Femme du Boulanger*, which painted attractive pictures of Marseille and its environs. Pagnol had a knack for shining a spotlight on the Provencal way of life at its best. Characters in his films hadn't a care in the world and they indulged in the pleasures of sunny Provence, drinking pastis and eating daube and aioli. Between shots, actors would congregate under the trees to partake in a game of *pétanque*.

Provencal chansons were enjoying wide popularity as well thanks to the mellifluous voices of Vincent Scotto and Tino Rossi. France found that the *joie de vivre* of Marseille was infectious.

Meanwhile, the French were discovering their own country like they never had before. With the newly instituted paid vacations and less expensive train fares, more people were traveling.

Their first destination, especially if they lived in the dour climes of the north, was the sea and sunshine of the south coast. What better way to spend your holiday than sipping pastis and playing a game of *pétanque*? While visitors flowed into Marseille and its environs, the locals found work in a flourishing tourism industry. Paul concentrated all his energy on how to capitalize on the situation.

How best could he imprint the name Ricard in their minds? He took it as his mission to not only sell them his pastis, but also to sell them his name. Ricard knew the importance of brand recognition. In a crowded marketplace, the name that most easily found its way to customers' lips would win the war. It was pure logic. He was sure that customers would be faithful once they tasted his pastis. It was a quality product. But brand recognition played an equally vital role. The brand had to be evocative of an entire lifestyle and to spark his clients' imaginations with the values he associated with his drink: sun, conviviality, Provence, Marseille.

When his father was alive, Paul's publicity gambits remained modest in keeping with his father's conservative character. He tried mostly to drum up business by chumming around at bars and offering incentives to barmen to get people drinking his brand. Now that Joseph was gone, Paul was able to give his ambition free rein.

Poster from 1938.

He hired a deft letter painter and had all of his delivery trucks embellished with the Ricard name in the lemon yellow of the sun and sea blue. For Paul, the reference to the sun and sea were primordial. It was a psychological play—a subliminal message—he was sending to consumers' minds. He wanted them to see the Ricard name and feel the impulse to drink his pastis in order to feel the warmth of the southern climes of Provence. Blue and yellow had a visceral quality that Paul adored.

Paul's talent in marketing united with his uncanny ability to simplify a message, breaking it down to its essential components. The most obvious solution often proved to be the most effective. On the motorway near Lyon, for instance, he had the Ricard name painted on a 27-yard-long long wall. It was visible more than 500 yards away. The impact was meant to be big—and it was. It got people talking. Paul liked to generate brand noise. He looked for good spots to place his ads. One of his favorite ads blazoned a wall visible from a railway car. He reasoned that people had more time and energy to concentrate on his message while sitting in a train compartment than while driving a car.

Advertising in 1932 felt quaint by today's standards. The ubiquity of ads was hardly the same without television, not to mention today's new media. Mostly it was relegated to posters and other paraphernalia linked to the brand. Paul's guiding principle was to be seen and to work the terrain. His method was commonsensical. He believed his product would be loved once people tried it. The trick was to get them to try. He went into the streets. Much like the young men and women who spritz perfume on clients in a department store, Paul distributed testers of his aperitif in small bottles, known in France as *mignonettes.*

Evolution of labels for carafes. From left to right: 1967, 1969, 1976, 1978, 1984.

The more people he could get to taste his drink, the more clients he was sure to earn. He believed as much. Paul was naturally gregarious, a trait he thought typically Provençal, and connected easily with people. He was prone to monologues because he believed in the ideas that coursed through his brain. But that didn't seem to bother anyone. People liked him. They liked his drink. It was the same quality he looked for in his collaborators. They had to be likable. He sent them home if he wasn't satisfied with their attire. Paul never put much stock in his own dress. Although later in life he could afford fine tailored suits, he often trucked to the local supermarket to do his shopping, buying dozens of cheap shirts at a time. Dress was never anything he spent much energy perfecting in his own life, although he was always impeccably turned out.

Paul wanted to achieve utmost efficiency in his communication program. He created an in-house art department, and he even hired artisans to fashion the accessories with which to drink his aperitif, from glasses printed with the Ricard name to yellow ceramic pitchers used to pour the five volumes of water needed to dilute the pastis. Collectors today covet the earliest Ricard ceramics and glasses with keen interest. At the time, they complemented a complete Ricard branding environment from which to spread the name and bolster its mystique. What Ricard was doing was similar to what Coca-Cola had done in the United States, finding a unique bottle design and flooding consumers with matching paraphernalia.

Ceramic water pitchers.

Paul's talent for communicating directly with his clients spilled over to the taglines he used in print campaigns. They were direct, but highly evocative, as *Boire un pastis à la marseillaise,* or Drink Pastis the Marseille Way; or *Ricard, pour le patron,* or Ricard, for the Boss.

Yet some of Ricard's advertising still used the old connection between pastis and absinthe. One of these early ads, for instance, shows a barman in a white jacket pouring water through a perforated spoon with sugar over a drink. The tag line read: *Ah, moi je bois un Ricard.* The imagery was highly evocative of the outlawed absinthe drink. Paul wanted to win over those old clients.

As his drink gained in popularity and he could distance his image from the old guard, he started using tags to position his Ricard as the original pastis of Marseille. When, in 1938, Paul launched his first national ad campaign, he used the tag *Ricard, le vrai pastis de Marseille,* or Ricard, the real pastis of Marseille.

Paul felt confident enough now that his drink could stand alone and claim the title to the throne as local legend. The accompanying poster depicted a bottle and two glasses, one glass indicating how the drink should be dosed with water and a price of 1 Franc 75 cents. The yellow-and-white-striped beach parasol in the background was evocative of Marseille. Gone were the references to absinthe.

Ricard had established its own vocabulary, a vocabulary that the company would retain in many ways even to this day. Paul had distilled the essentials of his drink down to just a few key components. The two glasses showed that it was a drink to be shared. You didn't drink Ricard alone. Secondly, Paul wanted to educate his clients on how to drink his pastis, with five parts water to one part pastis. Third, price. Fourth, the colors that gave the ad's semiotics an indelible link to Marseille.

The first principle Paul fell back on was always simplicity. "Before doing advertising one must ask 'Will this increase sales?'" He spent long hours contemplating the intricacies of advertising and the most effective means to achieve his goal. He knew that companies with the financial brawn to pump into advertising would be able to sell more easily.

He recognized that advertising was often traditionally linked to discounts. But this is not how he wanted to align his ads. That strategy would be short-lived in his mind. A winning formula would involve creating an image for his brand. And that would take time.

"To keep the public's attention, advertising needs to give them what they expect."

Yet achieving the obvious required finesse.

"To succeed, one needs to be taken seriously," he said in a memo addressing his advertising strategy to his managers. "One must convince. One must not mystify the public by sensationalism that seems attractive but, very quickly, disappoints."

As an example, he alluded to an ad by a gas company that created a fake report about scientists that had been able to integrate a tiger in a motor. That type of fantastical banter did nothing but confuse the client as to the clarity of the message, Paul believed.

Paul launched a new form of advertising: editorial based on purveying so-called information. Its argument leaned primarily on public health and was geared both to consumers and café owners. He published a book, for instance, that included the history of pastis, tracing its antecedents back to antiquity. The book explained in detail how pastis should be consumed as well as its potential health benefits, including the easing of digestion.

"Pastis is a natural drink," reads one section of the book. "It has no chemicals. It is healthy because the licorice eases the stomach and the anis regularizes the functions of the intestine. A glass of pastis prepared with five volumes of water for one volume of pastis has less alcohol than a glass of ordinary wine of the same volume."

The book even contained food recipes using Ricard, including *escargots au Ricard* and *poulet ricardière*.

In 1939, Ricard advertising leaned on drinking it the Marseille way (with five parts water). It evoked the sun, the French Riviera, a special place in a sentimental atmosphere. In 1949, after ten years of being outlawed, the efficiency of this campaign paid off.

"Today's success is the result of yesterday's effort. Tomorrow's success will be the result of today's effort," said Paul.

Paul was passionate about advertising. He was an active participant in some of the earliest Ricard campaigns in that he used his own paintbrush to design posters and ads. Later, he felt himself

Paul Ricard painting his own posters, 1964.

to be the chief idea man behind the campaigns and laid out intricate guidelines by which he found advertising would be most effective.

These are some of the instructions that Paul laid out:

"In advertising, one must know to whom one is speaking. One must be on the same wavelength."

"One has to push a good brand image (comfort, joy, well-being)."

"One must start with the assumption that the public is not informed."

"A brand cannot exist by advertising alone, but advertising that supports a brand must adapt. Therefore one must realize the fact that 29 million French people can't read."

"Word of mouth communication, which is exercised in cafés, loses all interest due to the fact that after 7:30 in the evening, everyone is at home in front of a television."

"One must realize the differences in sensibility between one country and another. The argumentation must be adapted."

"Advertising is a presale service but it is not sufficient. One must be preoccupied by the interference between sales and advertising."

"It is impossible to try to convince the over-40 age group. Advertising must target the young adults. American advertising gives the impression of being 'simplistic' but that it is because it is addressing the mental level of a 14-year-old."

"An argument should be used until its saturation point. It should not be replaced once it is used."

"Information is essential not only about the products but the company: one is interested by the 'private life' of a company as well.

Our only enemies are those that don't know us."

"The argument of an ad should be cleared of all superfluous words. It should be as pure as a drawing."

"Don't remain open to interpretation. One must write what one wants to say."

Innovation underscored all of Paul's beliefs. After the war, for example, Paul saw a stellar opportunity in hitching his name to a film by Marcel Pagnol called *Manon des Sources*.

Typically Provençal in its story of struggle and destiny set among the craggy hills around Marseille, Pagnol's epic film, later remade by Claude Berri, was exactly the type of vehicle Paul sought for his brand.

He dispatched one of his employees to the set with twenty metallic advertising placards that were promptly positioned in front of a café.

Pagnol was a little worried that it looked quite heavy-handed, but the director took it good-naturedly. So much so that a Ricard ad plays center stage in the first scene of the film, where a group of men are bantering around a table.

After all, what was a café in Provence without Ricard paraphernalia?

Paul took a large amount of inspiration from the communication strategy of one of his idols, André Citroën, who had built one of France's most successful automobile empires from scratch.

Citroën knew the importance of engraving his brand on the minds of potential clients and did not shy from spectacular stunts. He had an airplane write his name in the sky above Paris on one occasion. On another, he sent cars in an expedition across the Sahara desert that was retold in cinemas across France. Perhaps his most memorable stunt came in 1925, when he lit up the Eiffel Tower with a spectacular display of 200,000 lights and fireworks, his name blinking on and off in letters more than 30 yards high.

Attracting attention required big guns and a big budget. Paul was ready to deploy any means necessary. Pastis was a battleground that needed to be won in the minds of the clients. Ricard's biggest rival was Pernod, which seemed to have a head start in the biggest market in France: Paris.

Paul knew that Paris was the crown jewel in the market and that he would have to redouble his efforts if he were to convince the jaded Parisian consumer to drink his pastis. France was split between two worlds: Paris and the provinces. Highly centralized around the capital were all of the main corporate and government offices. In Paris, the aperitif market was virgin territory. There was no ancestral habit of drinking pastis as in Marseille.

Paul knew it would prove difficult to attack Pernod on the quality front. Quite the opposite. Taking a page from one of his boyhood idols—Henry Ford—Paul decided it would be by democratizing his product. His image was to be inclusive. Not elitist.

Paul's staggering success in Marseille and elsewhere in Provence startled the competition. They didn't like his atypical success and his way of inviting clients to drink less—at least in appearance—with a small dose of alcohol diluted with water. Pernod took Ricard's success as a menace to its own.

Paul had done the math in his head. If with a liter of his pastis a bar were to sell 50 drinks at 1 franc rather than 13 drinks at 2 or even 3 francs, the profits would be much greater. Paul wanted the bars behind his product. Making them more money was a surefire way to do so.

Pernod, however, had a considerable head start in reaching the hearts of the average Parisian drinker. In their attempt to steal business from Ricard, they had launched a hugely successful advertising campaign based around a fictional character named Arthur. Dressed in a bow tie, bowler hat, and mustache, Arthur was meant to represent the average Frenchman and to appeal to a desire to drink what everyone else was drinking. The ads met with incredible appeal and Arthur became one of the best-recognized characters in the French ad market.

Needless to say, Paul hated Pernod's ads and everything that he took Arthur to represent. He saw the incarnation of Arthur as mediocre and vulgar and did not hesitate to say so. Paul was cognizant of the strengths he could build on: sun, sea, Provence, its accent, the growing vogue for holidays, and the Provençal way of life. When he met with the advertising executive he had hired at the Havas agency, Paul beat it into his head that he wanted to channel the "soul" of his product.

Founded by Henri-Louis Pernod in 1805, Pernod company had been the most important distributor of absinthe, operating (close to 30 absinthe distilleries) at the height of the drink's popularity. When the drink was outlawed, Pernod also recognized the potential of an anise-based drink and, like Paul, launched one in 1938 when the government repealed the ban. Pernod, with its established manufacturing muscle and distribution network presented Ricard with its stiffest competition. But the upstart Paul, with his determination, quickly deserved serious attention. Competition between the two firms would continue for years, and—much later—end in marriage.

Paradoxically, the two great competitors shared the same advertising agency, with account executives only doors away from each other in Paris. Ultimately the combat between the two firms would spill over to the advertising colleagues, who would have a memorable falling out.

Paul knew that Paris was not Marseille and that he couldn't employ the same pavement-beating methods he had there to drum up business. Nonetheless, he did plan to align himself with all the owners of bars and restaurants hailing from Marseille. He wanted to build on the theme that his pastis was to be drunk the Marseille way.

His ad executive didn't think that was strong enough to be considered advertising. Paul insisted. He wanted to personalize his approach. "It's impossible to tell people to eat this or drink that because it is the best," he said. "The product needs a soul."

If Pernod had Arthur, Paul had Darcelys, who sang songs about Marseille and the Provençal lifestyle. There couldn't have been two more different approaches to selling two similar products. Instead of telling people he was the best, Paul wanted his product to sound in their mind like a song. When they drank his Ricard, when they felt it smooth over their palate, they could imagine themselves playing a round of *pétanque* under the warm Mediterranean sun.

Paul's strategy began to pay dividends. Sales in Paris grew swiftly and soon he had to move out of the depot he had opened in the city center to a larger one on the outskirts, in Pantin. Paul spent long hours poring over the strategy with his ad executive. Together they brainstormed, filling pages of paper with ideas. Paul wanted to distill all of his drink into the most succinct of messages. His favorite was the most direct: *"Garçon, un Ricard!"*

The success of pastis in Paris was cemented. Business was humming in Sainte-Marthe and Paul thought that the future looked incredibly bright. But success sometimes comes with a price. The anti-alcohol lobbies in France were raising their voices against the aperitif culture that had gained such traction. Anti-alcohol lobbies began entreating the government to raise measures against the likes of Pernod and Ricard. At the moment, in 1939, there seemed little reason to heed their entreaties.

Who could have imagined that in the next year the world would fall apart?

Paul Ricard interpreting his father in a tasting session from the movie *Nul Bien sans Peine*, 1964.

Chapter Five

THE OUTBREAK OF WAR PRESENTED PAUL with several issues he had to deal with. First, he was at the head of a company with 600 employees, many of whom were men. Suddenly, these men were conscripted into the army, as was Paul himself. Continuing the business in such circumstances would prove very challenging, if not impossible. Paul had received orders to report to duty. Running a company from the barracks could prove to be more than even the energetic and optimistic Paul could manage.

There was little love lost between Paul and the French military. During his obligatory service, Paul had butted heads with top brass. For a man orchestrating a fast-growing business, the subservience of military life held little appeal. One particular incident earned Paul the animosity of his commanding officer. Paul had refused orders to go on maneuvers and move machine guns without the mules. The absurdity of carting guns off on his back in order to please a man's whim was anathema to Paul. It was beyond his logical stacked head to blindly follow orders. It kept him from bowing to rank. Paul was a maverick, unafraid to speak his mind or follow his impulses. Obviously, he was not cut out for military life. Also, he was used to being the boss himself. He would never impose an impossible task on his workers. Why should he accept them when doled out by others?

Paul didn't mind work, even physical effort. What he never understood was wasted energy. With the help of a truck, he could fulfill the order easily. Yet his commanders wanted it executed immediately—and on their terms. Naturally Paul refused to subject himself to what he thought was cruel and unusual punishment for a task that could be completed without pain.

On another occasion, Paul poked fun at the captain in front of a general. Captain Campocasso, the commanding officer, would never forgive him. Paul had a quicker mind than most of his commanders. If they were intent on humiliating him physically, he would do the same mentally. The bad blood between Campocasso and Paul lingered long after the war. Years later, Campocasso's father and cousin, who had a bistro, refused to serve Paul's pastis. It was a fact that Paul found more amusing than vexatious.

This time, however, the stakes were different. Everyone knew that this was real war. Few, however, saw the start of the war as a prelude to the conflict of epic proportions that would play out over years, cost countless lives, and cause long strife and suffering. Most thought it would be brief, a passage of some weeks or months. It would be an interlude that the men could reflect fondly upon later in life. When Paul received his summons for duty, the gravity of the situation remained misunderstood.

Reports in the papers and radio failed to paint the events as dire as they were. The German invasion of Poland had elicited declarations of war from Poland's French and British allies. But nothing seemed to happen after that. A waiting game ensued. German troops appeared stagnant and neither the French nor British showed any appetite to charge in. War was declared, but no one took action. The allies wanted to avoid it. And most thought that this state of inaction would become the new normal.

In the beginning of May 1940, only weeks before German tanks rolled into Paris and right on the heels of the Reich's *Blitzkrieg* troops marching into Denmark, Norway, the Netherlands and Belgium, Paris appeared oblivious to the looming danger.

Government safety measures were only taken once Germany invaded France on May 14, 1940. Cars were forbidden to leave Paris and many people were relegated to going to work on foot or on the rare buses that had not been commandeered by the army to transport troops to the front.

Paul tried to keep up with the situation from his outpost in the south, mostly through letters and the odd verbal report delivered through messengers. Company managers continued to dispatch trucks back and forth from Ricard's depots on the outskirts of Paris to deliver his drinks to clients in the city center. It was difficult for Paul to decipher more. Letters from staff were his only source of information, and those were sporadic.

Looking back on some of those letters provides an interesting lens on the mood of the time.

One exchange of letters between Parisian management and Paul in Marseille is particularly telling. Business was suffering in Paris.

People were afraid and didn't feel like going out. Orders stagnated, but the manager of Ricard's warehouse just north of Paris, in Pantin, wrote, in a letter dated May 16, 1940, (ten days after Hitler invaded France) that, "Nonetheless, there is no panic in Paris, although everyone is on guard and ready to flee at the first serious alert."

He continued, "It is my personal impression that if the (German) advance is stopped in its path, the Paris area will not move and will see confidence improve for the great benefit of our business. But in the case of an improbable terrible blow, you can count on me to protect your interests."

The letter not only shows optimism but also the supreme loyalty that Ricard's employees had for their boss.

In a letter a month later, on June 14—the day the Germans entered Paris—the manager says that the staff's general sentiment was that the situation would find a rapid resolution. In the letter, he explains that the head of Ricard's operations had disappeared and that no one knew his whereabouts. But that business would go on. "Our brand is well enough known to be sold well if we set our minds to it."

After Nazi troops overran Paris and French leadership capitulated to the Third Reich, Ricard's business in Paris came to a grinding halt.

Running a company in the midst of war was a daunting task. Running it by proxy—and without the help of able-bodied men, all of who were summoned to report to duty—proved simply impossible.

Paul was told to report to Pertuis, then to Crest, in the Drome region, where his father-in-law Dr. Louis Thiers practiced medicine. Most of Paul's comrades were convinced he had, through influence, been dealt a favorable posting, close to family. In reality, he had done nothing of the sort. Fortune had smiled upon him.

For his first tour in the military, during his military service, Paul spent ten months as a sergeant in charge of mail delivery. "It was the best post," he said. "You knew everyone and you are really popular because you come bearing letters, packages, and orders."

Upon his return to active service he was reinstated to those responsibilities. He had seven days to join the regiment to which he was assigned. Paul decided that he would make the journey in the truck emblazoned with Ricard's yellow and blue colors. The vehicle had been transformed into a makeshift, rolling hotel, with a small salon, bunk beds, and a shower. It was quite a sight: a mobile home à la Ricard that announced Paul's arrival with fanfare. Even under the threat of war, Paul wanted to promote his brand.

The truck so impressed Paul's commanding officer that it was requisitioned as his own office upon Paul's arrival. Paul didn't seem to mind. It was all in the spirit of Ricard!

Chasseurs Alpins, Military Service, 1930.

No one seemed interested in fighting. Most soldiers passed the time by talking about what was to come. They wondered about the safety of their families. Would Germany really be as bad of a foe as some feared? Paul found himself among soldiers who did not know what to do. It was not a state of affairs he liked—or was used to. Paul liked accomplishment. The first days of the war were a painful and seemingly eternal waiting game. The orders from Paris were to bide their time. Most people believed that the war would end as it had started: quickly. No one had any appetite for a drawn-out conflict.

For a man who had become accustomed to managing scores of men and women, the task of delivering mail was rudimentary to Paul. It took little time and effort, mental or physical. By mid-morning he had completed his duties and had the entire day before him. Paul fell back on his old passion for painting. He needed to exercise his mind. He strapped an easel on his back and hiked out into the woods, where he would find solace in painting directly from nature. Paul was always at home alone in nature. He felt the grandeur of the mountainous landscape surge in his soul. Painting voraciously was what he liked. He tried to coax the colors from his palette to imitate what he saw. He had a literal approach to painting, but one that tried to boil down his subject into essential components. Paul liked painting people in particular because it was his way of deciphering what he thought he gleaned from their inner being. He believed the painter privileged, able to delve into the person behind the mask. Paul felt similar emotions when painting nature scenes. It allowed him a window on the deeper aspects of the world.

When he returned to the garrison after an afternoon painting, Paul sought the company of his fellow soldiers. He felt at peace. Paul was sociable and everyone liked him. He had a keen nose for picking up details in a person's personality. That attention to others earned respect. His comrades were all too happy to sit for a portrait. There was little else to do, and chatting with Paul while he sketched was not an entirely disagreeable prospect.

Paul wasn't alone in his artistic proclivities. One of his commanding officers was an instructor at the Beaux-Arts in Paris. One can only imagine his surprise when he walked into Paul's barracks to find some fifty portraits hung from the walls.

Paul's mother, Rose, had taken over the duties of guiding the company in Marseille. The war had taken all of the company's able-bodied men. Women were all who remained. Under Paul's mother's direction, these women orchestrated the tasks of fabrication, delivery, and management.

In Provence, the serious dangers of war had yet to set in as they had farther north, where the Germans had overrun Paris and elicited its surrender. Paul was still delivering mail, although that task proved more difficult with the arrival of hardened war. Paul's commanding officers tried to keep up a brave face. One told Paul his apartment in Paris was certainly occupied by Germans now, but that he should not lose hope of victory. Meanwhile, he sent Paul looking for the bags of mail that most probably had been left undelivered in train stations due to the current hardships. With his chauffeur, Paul drove furiously around Provence, from Aix to Valence.

Paul's company was set on the move. It seemed as if they were playing musical chairs, changing camps with no rhyme or reason beyond perpetual movement.

As the men grew restless, they recruited Paul to approach the commander for an explanation. They felt patriotism surging in their captain's chest. They wanted action and felt helpless biding time. Entering the office, Paul felt a heavy sentiment of hopelessness. "*Mon capitaine*, what are we waiting for? The Germans are overrunning the country."

With a sigh, the captain told Paul he needed to have faith in the strategy of the top brass. War, after all, is not run according to the initiatives of one man, he told Paul. There is a chain of command, with decisions ordered out through hierarchy. It was hardly the response that Paul wanted to hear. Reading between the lines, he saw that little was to come of their wartime exercises. He knew that returning to the men with such dour news would not improve their spirits.

Paul's commander, however, suggested he could prove useful to the gendarmes, who were organizing an operation to round up Italians. Mussolini had just declared war on France, just at the moment that the country was practically subjugated by the Germans.

What was to follow showed Paul just how terrible war could be. He followed the police to a village in the mountains where a so-called dangerous Italian foe was hiding out. When they arrived, guns in hand, the man in question didn't even know war had been declared. A big storm had knocked out the electricity and he had been unable to listen to the radio for days. Paul saw an innocent man being arrested.

Nearby his family was in tears.

Paul followed the police to Grenoble where they apprehended a bunch of young Italians living with their parents. Again, the men were stunned by their arrest. They were left crying in the street as they waited to be transported to prison. For Paul, the scene was ingrained in his memory. War brought out the animal in people.

War was so far removed from art. Later in life, he was asked what was most important for an industrial leader: art or technique? He answered art because one required imagination to build. For Paul, art was the mirror of civilization. It was the bulwark of the human soul against tyranny and oppression.

"Without artists, we would not be evolved because we would not have the education that artists give us," he said. "Like a tree, man needs roots. His roots are his past and enable him to resist storms. In order to make a better world, we must elevate man and give him dignity and elevate his soul with a better environment, one that is made and decorated for him by true artists. The harmony of their creation in turn will elevate his thoughts."

With the fall of Paris, an armistice was engineered between the Germans and the French. They divided the country in half between the occupied north and the so-called free-zone in the south that was to be governed by the Vichy puppet government in subservience to Germany.

As part of the armistice, the French military was disbanded. Paul's military life, spent mostly hanging around, biding time, ended as suddenly as it had begun. There were few other choices but to put down arms and return home. Now he would have to face the reality of operating a company in the most inauspicious of circumstances.

Paul found his company in disarray and steeped in uncertainty. There was little indication how occupation by Germany would play out for his business. Obviously, he knew it wouldn't be favorable. It didn't take long to learn just how unfavorable it would be.

On September 24, 1940, the government declared a formal prohibition on the production of all pastis in the whole of France, occupied or not. It felt as if all of the success that Paul had labored to achieve was crumbling around him. He was sitting at the bar Terminus in Sainte-Marthe when the news came over the radio: All drinks containing more than 16 percent alcohol were banned.

For Paul and his employees, the news resounded as loud as a German bomb. The men sitting with Paul could hardly believe their ears. A deafening silence fell over their group like a shroud. What would they do? How would they live? Besides the terrible fatality of living in the midst of de facto occupation by the Germans, the future had just turned even grimmer.

Paul was never one to roll over and play dead. His mind already had begun to calculate contingency plans. He figured that he could funnel part of the capacity at the factory into other products, including fruit juice, vermouth, and even alcohol-based fuel.

But that would never be enough to keep everyone at the factory employed. He had hundreds of employees. He felt responsible for their well being. He had organized his company as a family. And he was at the head. In a certain way he was their father. Now it was his duty to ensure their protection.

Keeping the factory running at some capacity would help ease the transition back to full-blown pastis production once the war ended, Paul reasoned, yet he needed to create another outlet for his employees. And for himself. Paul was not one to sit on his hands and bide time. Everything in his life hinged on creation. War represented the antithesis. Destruction was everywhere. He needed to fulfill a deep-rooted need to create.

As the radio continued to elaborate on the disturbing news of the law outlawing pastis, Paul stood up and circled around the table, examining the faces of his cohorts. They were silent and slouched in their chairs with their heads hung low.

"I'm a sore loser," Paul reasoned in his head. "There are two ways to react when everything seems to be crumbling around: lose your cool and curse your fate or rage against bad fortune with a good heart. Even if it doesn't change anything, keeping your head high reassures others that there is still hope. It's the only way to win at poker."

Paul never avoided gambling in order to win. He didn't like to lose, either. His risk-taking was calculated.

He demanded their attention. "My friends," he said, "We are going to be farmers."

Paul saw the disbelief on their astonished faces. Tilling the earth was far removed from brewing pastis. But Paul knew it could work. And he knew that it would prove important. If war continued, the country would need food. Basic necessities would become increasingly vital. Working the earth was a return to primal civilization. If the world around was consumed in barbarism, he would return to the basics. His farm would become an example of a civilized world amid the uncivilized.

Paul had purchased a large farm in the Camargue marshlands west of Marseille in 1939. At the time it was an investment like any other. The Camargue, covering 360 square miles of rugged, windswept marshland south of Arles, is Western Europe's largest river delta, where the Rhône, after running for 500 miles from Switzerland through France, spills into the sea. With more than a third of the land occupied by marshes, the Camargue has long been one of France's largest natural reserves, sparsely populated by humans, home to countless flamingos, wild horses, and bulls. The latter are among Europe's fiercest, renowned for their speed and cunning. They are particularly coveted for bullfighting. Even in Roman times the bulls of Camargue were considered the meanest and impossible to tame.

It is inhospitable land made for the toughest and most determined. The earth is heavy with salt, making cultivating crops and livestock challenging to say the least. And then there are the mosquitoes. In the summer months, when the humidity and heat soar, the insects swarm like bees on honey. It was a situation that, for the most part, kept all but the most resolute from living in the region.

Obviously, the difficulties of the land did not deter Paul. All challenges, particularly the most difficult, only served to whet his appetite. Now that war had suffocated his spirits business, he resorted to plan B.

His property was called Méjanes. It was what the French call a "domaine," somewhat akin to the American ranch, that most certainly first came into existence around the tenth century. It occupied a strategic post in close proximity to the ports of Saintes-Marie-de-la-Mer and Aigues-Mortes, both important launching points for boats heading to the Holy Land during the Crusades of the twelfth century. By the time of Louis XV, in the early eighteenth century, the heads of the estate had been ennobled as marquis by the king and taken the title of marquis de Méjanes.

Yet in 1939, the property was in utter disrepair. Its fields were fallow and too salty to cultivate. Wild horses roamed its swampy lands amid flamingos and the occasional bull. There was little to envy in its geography. Méjanes, like the whole of Camargue, had seen better days. During the first half of the nineteenth century, Camargue and the neighboring city of Arles were subjected to a series of debilitating floods. Napoleon III took it upon himself to correct the situation with a series of dykes designed to help regulate the flow of water between the Rhône and the sea. After a decade of steady work, the project had reached an end. But cultivating the earth in Camargue in wartime Europe remained daunting. With its high salinity, the earth required laborious washing via freshwater canals before it was even close to being called ready for cultivation.

It was no wonder that Paul purchased Méjanes cheaply. Only fifteen of its 1,200 hectares were cultivated (for grapes for cheap wine) when he signed the deed. At the time, he had no immediate use for the fields. His plan was to grow fennel, mint, and licorice, essential ingredients for his pastis. Paul was also attracted to the myth of Camargue. It was a land for brave men and women undeterred by difficulty and labor. He considered himself of that ilk. He also appreciated the wide-open spaces of the Camargue. The romanticism of the place appealed to his free spirit. When the wind isn't blowing and the mosquitoes are quiet, few places are as beautiful, with unimpeded vistas of natural splendor, punctuated by flocks of pink flamingos reaching for the sky against the golden horizon.

Paul's domaine de Méjanes had previously belonged to the Saint Louis sugar refineries and was used to cultivate beets during the First World War. Years had elapsed since the land had been used. Paul, an eternal optimist, was determined to make it yield to his will.

As he outlined his plan to his downtrodden employees, Paul sensed their disbelief. He needed to act quickly and decisively if he was to win their hearts so that they would follow his lead with the enthusiasm he knew that it would require.

With his typical steely determination, Paul bought forty milk cows and dispatched them in one of the last blue-and-yellow Ricard delivery trucks to Méjanes. The irony of the situation was lost on no one. Ricard's trucks were now transporting dairy! Those cows would hardly be enough to feed an entire nation, but they could provide milk for nearby schools.

Paul's intentions to diversify predated the war. Apart from Méjanes, he had purchased a mineral water source called Pestrin, located near the ancient volcanoes in the sparsely populated and rugged Ardèche region.

Legend had it that the source was discovered in the twelfth century by a troubadour whose master had left for the Crusades. When his master returned, the troubadour was said to serve the water to his tired master and his troops, ridden with illness and even plague. Rich in magnesium, zinc, and iron, the water was reputed to have cured them of all their ailments.

Paul decided to send part of his staff to Pestrin to oversee bottling and distribution of the water. By keeping a toe in the distribution business, he hoped that he would stay in touch with clients for when better times returned.

"Circumstances have forced us to change direction," he told his employees, adding that a part of the workforce would stay at the factory to keep up the daily cleaning and a small production of fruit juices.

He was unsure that they would have enough work to remain fully occupied or make enough money to be paid. Some of the others would be dispatched to Pestrin and the rest would come with Paul to Méjanes to cultivate the earth.

"First we will become masons to lodge ourselves and our beasts, then farmers to raise cows for milk and meat and to optimize the land of Méjanes. Our goal will be to nourish ourselves, as well as our families, and to help provide supplies to those in the region."

Vichy ordered Paul's factory to be closed for the "public good." Ricard hadn't expected any less. In restitution for the jobs lost, the Vichy government offered a month's pay to each of the employees—but not the boss—and required Paul to travel to Vichy himself to collect the reparations.

The wartime trip left a stern impression on Paul. Upon his arrival, he had to sleep in a chair in the hall of a hotel since all the rooms had been requisitioned for government use. Everything in Vichy seemed grey and sinister to Paul. The administration of capitulation sent shivers down his spine. The next morning he managed to wrangle a meeting with a functionary who again told Paul that he himself would not receive any reparations for the closure of his firm. He packed up his things. He couldn't wait to get home.

Plenty of challenges awaited his return.

A cult of Provençe was nurtured in Camargue at the beginning of the twentieth century. Women wore full colorful Provenççal regalia and men, dressed like gauchos, rode the most spirited of the locally bred horses. Frédéric Mistral, the great poet who wrote his verse in the Provençal dialect, was the model for reverence to the earth and traditions to which the staunchest believer adhered.

Many of these men and women were not pleased to catch wind of Paul's projects. They saw the industrialist as a big-city fat cat who would rip up the earth for temporary gain with no respect for the traditions they were so set on protecting.

The instigator for much of the local pride was the Marquis Folco de Baroncelli-Javon, a guardian, or a type of cowboy, who, though descended from Florentine aristocracy, spoke Provençal.

Baroncelli raised a herd of cattle known as the *Manado sentanco*, or the holy herd, on his farm. He devoted himself to raising pure-blood bulls and attained a mythical status close to god, in part, because of it. His guardians were deft riders. When they participated in a show of American cowboys and Indians led by Buffalo Bill during a visit to Nimes in 1905, the famous American cowboy was utterly impressed by their prowess in the saddle.

Baroncelli wanted to craft an identity for Camargue that aligned it with an idealistic, codified society apart from the savagery of the modern world. He wrote books extolling the characteristics of Camargue and captured its local folktales. He helped develop a local style of bullfighting in which the goal was to lift a rose from the bull's head. He wanted to bequeath a sense of individualism that set Camargue apart.

He felt uneasy with Paul's plans to carve a farm out of the marsh. Paul watched entranced as the marquis, perched majestically on his horse after riding into town in nearby Arles, returned home daily via Méjanes to his "mas" in Saintes-Maire-de-la-Mer. Despite his advanced years, the marquis spent at least eight hours a day in the saddle—always on the local Camargue-bred horses, which are the most difficult to tame.

Paul could read in the marquis' eyes his disapproval for what he wanted to achieve. Baroncelli thought that farming would desecrate the land he strove so hard to preserve. It would take away space for the wild roaming of animals. It would tame what he believed was best left unchained. Of course, this merely equated to a romantic version of reality. But Baroncelli, deep down, believed it.

As he watched Paul's renovations progress at Méjanes, Baroncelli began to warm to the project. He saw that, like himself, Paul was an idealist, a man bent on achieving the impossible in the midst of

Méjanes, 1960s.

adversity and that he held a deep respect both for the traditions of Camargue—and all Provençal traditions for that matter—as well as for those who strove to protect them.

One particular incident underscored Paul's commitment to preserving regional traditions. A great bronze statue of Frédéric Mistral was inaugurated in the Place du Forum in Arles in 1909. It was a symbol of pride for locals and the ultimate expression of their singular culture as expressed by their homegrown, Nobel Prize–winning poet.

Paul learned through friends that the Germans had designs to requisition the statue in order to melt down the bronze. He organized a group to clandestinely save the statue from destruction. In the dead of night, Paul led his band of raiders and they dismantled the sculpture from its base and hid it from the Germans. All during the war the sculpture was kept hidden. In 1948, it was returned to its rightful place.

Though Paul faced resistance from the locals, his biggest hurdles came from the land itself. It was inhospitable and the work involved ploughing the land so it could be turned into fertile fields was monumental. Several thousand tons of earth needed to be leveled in order to create an irrigation system that would use fresh water from the Rhone.

Paul called in a troop of workers from Tuscany who specialized in digging canals. They would be responsible for digging the irrigation canals that would allow him to bring in the fresh water needed to cultivate his crops.

The work was slow but sure. Each man managed to dig about nine cubic yards of earth during a seven-hour workday.

By growing rice, Paul managed to desalinate his lands. His first rice yields were encouraging, about 1 ton per hectare (about 2 ½ acres). To get anything close to optimum production, Paul would have to dig still more irrigation canals. Rice, in order to grow properly, needs some 35,000 tons of water per hectare. Although Paul's men were learning to grow rice, they had a lot to learn.

Paul and his workers still faced regular threats from the Germans. Troops would make regular visits with the intention of requisitioning any vehicles or tools they pleased. They took free rein of the food stores. Paul and his men created a watch system to alert the farm to a surprise visit. As soon as their sentry spotted the Nazis, the men scurried to hide the yield of the crops.

One afternoon turned particularly dangerous. A German airplane suddenly appeared on the horizon. The pilot opened fire on the fields. The men ran in disarray. Bullets ripped through a cow, leaving it bloody and dead on the field. For what? Luckily there were no other casualties.

The German threat came from elsewhere too. Many of Paul's younger workers were threatened with the possibility of having to leave for forced labor camps in Germany. Paul knew that if they left there was a chance they would never return. He paid a visit to his good friend Fernand Coder, another successful Marseille businessman, who ran a factory that made train cars. Under the German occupation, his workers had been exempted from forced labor as the Germans needed his industrial capacity in France. Coder told Paul there was no chance his agricultural employees would be exempt from work for the Germans. The two men schemed together to form a plan that they thought could work. When any of Paul's men received orders to report for labor in Germany, Coder would in turn hire them at his factories, fictitiously. It was risky, but the plan was successful. For other workers, Coder put Paul in contact with a German functionary in Marseille that he knew well. This particular official hated the Nazis and was married to a French woman. The German official told Paul he would help. Later, the German was shot for providing too many services to the occupied French.

Paul never hesitated to help men or women menaced by the

German threat. He knew, however, how dangerous it could be and tried to take as many precautions as he could to protect himself. His company in Pestrin was a propitious ruse. It was located in a remote area, mostly beyond the prying eyes of German surveillance. Paul began to hide people there. He procured false papers to travel anonymously under the name of Paul Roland. He was careful to keep his first name and his initials, so as not to give himself away by the monogram on his handkerchiefs or shirts or by a careless slip of the tongue. On his identity papers he listed his birthplace as Oran, Algeria, which was impossible to check now that the Americans had entered North Africa.

Hiding people proved to be a difficult business. When it came to Paul's attention that one of his Jewish army pals who operated the Galeries Lafayette department store in Nîmes was at risk of being deported to Germany, he sent word that his friend should meet him in Méjanes. Paul planned to help his friend and his family by dispatching them to Pestrin, where they could work at the source and keep a low profile.

Paul appointed his friend director of the water factory and all went well to start with. It was not long, though, before Paul received a frantic phone call informing him that his friend had been seized by a group of collaborators who forced him to turn over money from the safe and then detained him and his family, including two children.

There was little Paul could do in the face of this tragedy. He knew chances were incredibly slim that he would ever see his friend again. Indeed, the entire family never returned, after being sent to German concentration camps.

Paul knew now he could trust no one. There was always someone who could utter an indiscreet word. Too many people worked at Pestrin and Méjanes to completely control the situation. Utter secrecy would now be required in all his efforts to shelter the persecuted. Very few people could be trusted, and those few belonged to his utmost inner circle. Paul sent the remaining Jews he was hiding at Pestrin away to stay with a sympathetic farmer deep in the countryside. Later, the same group of Jews was forced to live in even remoter circumstances in the mountains. Fortunately, the despicable German machine failed to round them up.

As the war grew in severity, Paul needed to exercise more discretion in his help of anyone susceptible of being deported. His wife urged him to be cautious. He followed that advice on more than one occasion, declining offers to help some. It was becoming too well known that Paul was amenable to hiding people needing safe haven. On other occasions, however, Ricard couldn't turn down those he felt desperately needed his help. Some he helped to infiltrate the underground Maquis movement or the rural resistance guerilla fighters, which was mostly made up of men who had fled to the mountains to avoid conscription into forced labor in Germany. Ricard kept up to date on this underground resistance ring without direct participation. He felt that his contribution was to keep the men and women under his responsibility fed and safe. Paul was growing more worried that his phone was ringing a little too often in connection with the Resistance.

As the situation started to turn in the Allies favor, the war in Marseille and its environs became more dangerous for civilians. The Anglo-American bombings of Marseille on May 27, 1944, alone left more than 3,000 civilians dead. Paul took his family to Pestrin, where his team had close relations with the men of the Maquis. They would be safe there until the fighting ended. Victory was not far off. Paul started dreaming of peace. Finally, he could start to rebuild what the years of fighting had destroyed.

Paul Ricard in Méjanes in the 1950s.

Chapter Six

WITH THE DECLARATION OF PEACE, Paul's attention quickly returned to his pastis. How soon would he be able to reopen his factory? Life during the war had been taxing. He had done better than most by funneling his energy into the creation of the farm at Méjanes. But having been stripped of what he cherished most had weighed on his mind. Restarting his business now consumed his whole imagination. There was no more time to waste. He resolved to travel to Paris to find out when the government planned to repeal the Vichy-instituted laws banning anise-based drinks. He was convinced that it was only a matter of time.

Travel was complicated. The rail service was far from being restored and flying was completely out of the question. In the days, weeks, and even months after the war, survival itself was difficult. Finding food could be challenging. Travel by car to Paris proved the only viable option. The only automobile available had not been used in four years and had even been partly dismantled by Paul, who had removed and concealed its wheels to keep it from being requisitioned by the Germans. It would be easy enough to repair, however.

Paul loaded the back seat with cans full of fuel and set off for

Paris, accompanied by two friends.

After years of war, the roads were treacherous and parts of them had been completely bombed out. If Paul were to take the road through Avignon he would have to navigate all of the destroyed bridges along the Rhône. Many had been replaced by floating bridges that were dangerous and necessitated long waits behind massive queues of trucks, and parts of the road were completely untenable. Instead, Paul plotted an itinerary farther to the east.

The scenes of ruin along the road were incredible. Towns had been reduced to rubble and the countryside laid to waste by the rampage of battles. The desolation weighed heavy on Paul's heart. Such beautiful countryside had been part of his innocence and youth. Since he had been a little boy, driving had been one of his great pleasures. From the days of driving alongside his father in the backcountry of Provence, the motion of an automobile gave him deep satisfaction. As he drove on, he thought of his father and the many adventures they had started together. He felt an obligation to resuscitate Ricard and take it beyond its prewar success. He owed it to his father. He owed it to himself. And he owed it to his employees.

As he sped along, he heard a loud crack. The car screeched to a halt as Paul pulled over onto the shoulder. The car's wheel shaft had broken in two.

Finding a garage was not easy and, when he did find one, he was told that they didn't have replacement parts. But the mechanic told Paul not to lose hope. During the war the mechanic's father had buried spare parts to hide them from German soldiers. The only problem:

the mechanic's father was not due home from Paris for a couple of days and he didn't know where they were.

Paul waited.

After a couple of days of terrible boredom, Paul found someone to weld the wheel shaft together. The mechanic warned that the repair might not last. Undeterred, Paul drove on. Miraculously the car survived the pothole-ridden road and made it to Paris. Upon arrival, Paul set about his goal to meet the right politicians to learn when he would be able to revive his firm. Paul was astonished with the state of affairs in Paris. How he had misjudged his ambitions! No one was even close to being interested in listening to his entreaties. There were other more pressing problems to be dealt with first. France was in ruin. People had no food. Pastis was the last of their worries.

As Paul drove from one of his meetings, the inevitable arrived. The repaired wheel shaft broke again, this time irreparably.

With little hope, Paul jumped on a bus to go to the Renault factory on the western outskirts of the city to find the part needed to repair the car. When he arrived, he was shocked to find the factory shuttered. Paul had been so concentrated on his own quest that he had failed to understand just how bad things had become.

Louis Renault had been imprisoned, charged as a German collaborator for supplying tanks to the Third Reich's war machine. Paris was frantic with animosity and destruction. As Paul turned away from the deserted factory, he knew that it would be a long time before he would be able to reopen his company.

Under the hardship of conflict and Nazism, Paul had managed

to forge a life for himself at his rice farm in Camargue. There was a certain solace in knowing that he was not incapable of making ancillary schemes work in his favor. Even more satisfying for a man who liked to contribute to the well-being of others was that he had succeeded in creating jobs for people desperate for a livelihood in a time of dire need.

By the end of the war, in 1944, he was cultivating 20 hectares for rice. Just a year earlier, there had been no seeds available due to depravation from war. Paul was nothing if not determined. He produced 60 tons of rice the last year of the war and was well on his way to creating a totally independent farm. Furthermore, Paul had achieved something even greater: he had created *ex nihilo* a functioning parallel society—and a civilized one at that—in the

First rice paddy crop in Méjanes, 1943.

midst of the barbarism of Hitler's Reich. His farm in Méjanes had a school, housing for workers, and a regulated life. The people he had transplanted to Méjanes to make it function were fed. They had jobs. In the chaos of war Paul had given them a purpose. He had created a world of his own.

It was an achievement of which he was very proud. He would never abandon Méjanes. In fact, he wanted it to flourish into a serious agricultural concern. With the armistice, Paul had access to tractors and other machinery impossible to procure during combat. He got his hands on motor graders left behind by the Americans, which allowed him to dig more efficiently than ever, shoring up an entire freshwater irrigation system with 13 miles of new canals linked directly to the Rhône River. Meanwhile, the same machines facilitated the evacuation of brackish water via another fifteen-and-a-half miles of canals toward the Vaccarès, the largest lake in Camargue and an important home for pink flamingos.

Paul loved the lake, which bordered his property. Part of it belonged to Paul according to the deeds and the geographical position of Méjanes. He set up a fishing cabin on the lake where a single fisherman fished for eel year-round, subsisting from the catch alone. Most of the eel were sent to Italy, as the French have less taste for the delicacy.

Upon his return to Marseille, Paul didn't lose sight of his desire to engineer the return of a legal pastis trade. He took to lobbying local politicians. It didn't take long for the government to reauthorize the production of liquor at 40 percent alcohol. But that did him little good. Pastis needed 45 percent alcohol.

It seemed as if the government was intent on promulgating Vichy's wartime anti-liquor laws. Whereas Vichy had instituted them for one set of reasons, the new government in Paris had an entirely different agenda. It is true that the penury of alcohol had diminished alcoholism significantly during the war. Chronic alcoholism fell 75 percent during the war, while liver ailments dropped 57 percent. Other factors were at work, of course, but this stark reduction in alcoholism in France sent a clear message to politicians that alcoholism could be reduced through strict alcohol control.

Paul had to content himself with waiting. He had other means to make a living for himself and his employees, as he had proved during the war.

He dove headfirst into fashioning schemes for the promotion of his rice. It was as if he was imitating his younger self when he traveled bar-to-bar promoting his pastis. A potent way to promote his rice was to have it served on the popular cruise liners of the Compagnie Générale Transatlantique. He offered more than 200 pounds of free rice to serve on their ships. Tourists, he reckoned, would learn to love rice on board. Just like his farm and his distillery, the Transatlantique was reconstructing a fleet decimated by war. Paul knew that ultimately the new liners would represent just the level of glamour he wanted to associate with his rice.

Food was still scarce in the months after the war. He edited various tracts extolling the nutritional value of rice. Recipes were published as well. As with his pastis, Paul strove to explain his product to the consumer. Parallel to these activities, Paul ramped up his production of fruit, planting an additional 7,000 pear trees between 1944 and 1956 over some 14 hectares. He added an additional 5 hectares of plum and apple trees. These fruit orchards provided a good return on his investment.

For all the satisfaction that Paul found in his agricultural activity, he wanted more. There was a certain arbitrariness in the choice that he didn't like. Paul had been forced into the role of farmer, but Paul was a man who liked to impose his will. To have success dictated by circumstances did not seem the ultimate expression of his drive.

At home, his family was growing. After Danièle, who was born in 1938, Paul had another five children: Bernard, Betty, Patrick, Michèle, and Jean-Pierre, who was born with Down's Syndrome and died at the age of five.

Méjanes in 1939 (left). Paul and Marie-Thérèse and their children Danièle, Bernard, Béatrice, Patrick, Michèle, and Jean-Pierre in 1954.

The family cared for the sickly Jean-Pierre by sending him to the mountains where a nurse tended to his every need. Paul, obviously, was affected by his young son's death, feeling all the sadness of losing one of his own. But his wife took the blow harder. After the death of her youngest son she was never the same, something that did not go unnoticed by the family.

Already Paul was rarely home. Business kept him traveling constantly and working until late. He liked to have the family together for special occasions and was particularly attached to family meals. Yet he was a distant presence. Often he took to communicating with his children through letters, encouraging them to learn and to perform well at school. At times, Paul proved to be an absent father. Later in life, he admitted as much. In fact, he almost felt obliged to compensate for the fact by devoting long hours to his grandchildren, whom he coddled with gifts and attention. During the summer he organized long boat trips for his children's children, sailing with them and a small crew on his boat.

They toured the Mediterranean from France to Italy and Spain. Paul took his grandchildren to Pompeii and Napoli. Paul always mixed business and pleasure. He took his secretary Danielle de Petris and sometimes invited children from the family of one of his managers to accompany his own grandchildren on the voyage. Meetings were arranged during the trips to keep tabs on business and to promote Ricard. Paul's notion of family extended to his company—sometimes his grandchildren felt little difference between the work family and the blood family. But Paul devoted time to his grandchildren religiously.

Though he was not effusive and was often a quiet presence, he delighted them with presents. He offered encyclopedias or the latest electronic gadget, he himself being very interested in cameras and film. When the grandchildren were at the dinner table, Paul listened attentively, correcting a misconstrued fact or offering counsel. When one of his grandchildren asked a question that he was unable to answer, he would later look into the matter and offer a solid answer the next day.

His wife participated little in these scenes, and it was rare that Paul and Marie-Thérèse were together. They never divorced, but they lived separately, mostly uniting at family gatherings at Christmas and Easter. Mamie, as the grandchildren called Marie-Thérèse, remained a shadow figure in the house.

The Ricard clan gathered at Méjanes every Christmas. Their parties were lively and noisy. Paul distributed money, which his grandchildren appreciated for the obvious reasons. The men often received electric shavers. Paul was generous with his family, as he was with his employees. It was in his nature. He went to great pains to treat all his children and grandchildren equally.

Holiday Center Sausset les Pins, 1940s (left). Mister and Mrs Paul Ricard with their children and grandchildren, Bendor Island, 1964.

Paul was not demonstrative with his emotions. It was a question of generation in many respects. Many in the prewar generation considered emotions a personal affair. Paul had been through hardship and had always managed to overcome them through perseverance. He did not need to be effusive. He did not enjoy unnecessary conversations nor was he prone to chitchat. He liked to listen and was highly attentive with everything and everyone around him.

He expressed himself in other ways.

By the late 1940s, Paul branched into the business of making films. He had always been fascinated with celluloid. He snapped pictures constantly and filmed on his handheld Pathé Baby camera. To have his own studio would not only fulfill a passion, it could be a useful promotional tool for his pastis. He purchased some left-over material from Marcel Pagnol and built a massive studio on his property in Sainte-Marthe as well as a huge atelier for building sets.

Paul Ricard Cinema Studios, 1952. (Protis Society)

Paul inaugurated the studios to great fanfare in 1952 with a party for 800 people. His intent was to make a French Hollywood in Marseille. In fact, he travelled to Hollywood himself to get a better idea of the tenacious competition between the Hollywood studios and the tools he would need in order to succeed.

He produced and distributed a film by director Jacques Dary, *La Maison du Printemps*, the story of four girls who fall in love with the same man, which met with some success. In 1953, he launched a film he wrote himself: *La Caraque Blonde*, loosely based on Romeo and Juliet. Set in Camargue during the war, Paul substituted a family of rice farmers and another of cowboys for Shakespeare's Montagues and Capulets. The story came from his heart and his experience. It was a great success.

Paul was voracious and unable to deal with idleness. Unsurprisingly, he lived a highly regimented life. Later in life, when he retired to his mountaintop compound in Signes, in the wild boulder-pocked hills above Bandol, it was as if he had constructed the house to match his lifestyle. The great room was at least 100 yards long, like a corridor, lined with bookshelves and what could be described as individual workstations with desks. Paul used each desk for a different activity, one for correspondence, another for editing film or writing checks. A whole room along the corridor was used as a painting studio. He made his way down the rooms during the day as if he were working an assembly line.

Paul believed everything was possible through industry. It was a philosophy that he tried to impart to his grandchildren as well as his employees. No idea was a bad one. He forced self-confidence on people, extolling them to make a new friend every day. He believed in the force of numbers. He knew that self-confidence was infectious.

Company literature that he distributed to the sales team told them to kick off the blues by looking themselves in the mirror and telling themselves that they were the best salesmen of the best product in the world. He treated them as an effective coach may treat a world-class athlete, recognizing which buttons to push to get the best out of his player. He published a company broadsheet called Flash Ricard. It contained short editorials that imparted his keys for success to the company's employees. Paul believed that motivation lay in implicating his employees in the total well-being of the company. The more they were kept informed of key developments, the more they would work in the company's favor.

Later, he would provide tapes giving company information for salesmen to listen to during their long car trips across France. Point by point he instructed them on how to sell Ricard pastis. Paul overlooked no detail, including sartorial tips and encouraging salesmen to pay the utmost attention to their appearance, with perfectly pressed trousers, shirts, and clean-cut hair.

Rousing emotions was Paul's specialty. After each work meeting, the men would raise and sing a hymn to Ricard's pastis:

Ô toi, Sainte-Marthe
Reine du Pataclet
Sers, avant qu'on ne parte
Un bon Ricard bien frais.

Ave, ave, ave cinq volumes d'eau (Bis)

Aux hyponcondriaques,

Tu redonnes la joie

Tu préviens les attaques

Et les crises de foie.

Ave, ave, ave cinq volumes d'eau (Bis)...

These scenes showed that Paul had turned Ricard into a religion, with its own hymn. The atmosphere was virile and the men loved the camaraderie. It was not uncommon for Ricard men to break into the song at the end of a long work dinner. Then, after a few drinks, the song felt bacchanalian.

Paul did not only issue instructions to salesmen—advice was administered throughout the chain of command. In a memo to the deliverymen, for instance, he outlined the importance of their role. Every man, no matter his position, reflected the firm. "Delivery is the prolongation and culmination of a sale," he wrote.

"The battle, since sales is a battle, does not end when the sales representative leaves. The latter created a climate, an ambience, that continues a few days later when you arrive, not as an encore, but to collect the money. The scene is no longer the same. 'My husband is not here,' or 'I don't have the checkbook,' or 'Come back tomorrow.' Your role is not always easy, and we know it. You are parked outside in a loading zone. It's why you need to know how to comport yourself."

"Remember that the client judges our company through your appearance."

Paul told the deliverymen how they should speak, with

confidence, looking the client in the eye. "Be polite. Greet on entrance. Adopt a dignified and correct attitude."

Many of these lessons Paul gleaned when he had done deliveries himself at the beginning of his career.

"Once a week, I went to one of the neighborhoods of Marseille," he recalled. "I took my father's car, and I made a point to tip my hat and shake hands with the workers, customers, and owners of the bars, who were all flattered that someone with a car, wearing a tie, was shaking their hand because, at the time, having a car made you someone."

"Prestige, decorum, respect: they helped me sell. Whereas the salesman who arrived at the bar with a cigarette perched on his lip, who was too familiar with the clients, was doomed to failure."

His most innovative company information scheme came when he began to record film broadcasts with Yves Mourousi, the most famous of France's television newsreaders. Every month a video was provided to employees. They were also invited to conferences on such diverse economic subjects as credit or the intricacies of agriculture.

Paul felt a strong sense of family. When his wife's brother was killed during the war, he took in his two sons and treated them as his own. He set up a school for the children in Méjanes and felt strongly that they should get "real" experience as well as formal learning. He hired an in-house instructor to teach the children the basics of grammar and mathematics "in the old way," which he felt was more in touch with "reality." He was proud that his daughter Betty lent credence to his method when she could read almost perfectly at the young age of four.

Teaching his children English was one of his priorities. Paul, who knew his way around the modern business world, was convinced that language was of primordial importance in a modern education.

Paul sent his first son Bernard away to boarding school at St. Gall in Switzerland at 14 in order to learn German (and to open his mind to the world). Paul privileged action over sitting in a schoolroom, however. He based the projects he cooked up for his children on his own experience, which was one of trial and error and a keen understanding of human nature, which he valued so highly in all of his business transactions.

It was of little surprise when Paul organized a trip to Africa for Bernard. His son, with the supervision of one of Paul's advisors, would travel across a good chunk of Africa in a Citroen 2cv car!

One afternoon over lunch in 1956, Paul asked Bernard if he would like to visit Africa. Paul knew that the continent provided multiple opportunities for Ricard and that Bernard, whom he assumed would one day be his successor, should be primed to better understand the market.

Bernard did not resemble his father at all. With his blue eyes and clear complexion, he was the yin to Paul's yang, with the traits of his mother's side, the Thiers. He was excessively timid and not very good with people. He went to great lengths to please his father and counter his nature by trying to be extroverted.

Paul dispatched his son on what amounted to a rudimentary road trip, with little of the comforts he had become accustomed to at home. Bernard would sleep in a tent under the stars and report back to his father in a detailed 100-page report about his experience.

After a four-month, almost 400-mile trek through the bush, Bernard returned home exhausted. He continued his education and grooming with a trip to England and a six-month internship at Philips and the stock exchange in New York.

The relationship between eldest son and father went through its share of permutations, as could be expected from a father who demanded as much from his son as he demanded from himself.

Paul and his son Bernard on Bendor Island, 1952.

In fact, Paul expected all of his children to earn their stripes. He sent Patrick, his second son, abroad as well. Patrick, more at ease with people than his older brother, studied for two years in Heidelberg, then in Montreal, and finally did an internship with I.B.M. in New York. For Paul, it was a means of getting his son up to speed to manage the multi-national company Ricard was becoming.

His youngest daughter, Michèle, took her father's exhortations for self-sufficiency to a level he did not expect when she told her father that she planned to move to England and to live with no pecuniary help from him. She was hired to work as an au pair (although it didn't take long for her employers to realize her true identity).

As was the case in the early 1930s before the drinks were legalized, the months following the end of the war produced a clandestine market for pastis. The people of Provence would not live without their drink. As previously, the black market operated under little control.

Bootleggers dropped kegs of liquor into the sea from ships as they sailed close to Nice, Toulon, and Marseille. Under the stealth of night, men disguised as fishermen sailed out to collect the kegs, returning to port with a very lucrative haul.

With no strict control, the quality of the alcohol diminished. Some bootleggers used dangerous industrial alcohol in their concoctions. Anything they could obtain to brew their liquor in the lean postwar economy was employed. Police and customs measures were insufficient to stave off the trade. There was too much money to be made.

The situation was unsettling. Moreover, any attempts to convince officials to legalize pastis fell on deaf ears. This was incomprehensible to Paul. Wine was allowed, as were spirits, particularly whisky, which was enjoying a growing vogue thanks to the image it conjured of the

American liberators of France and Europe as well as its association in the popular psyche with the increasingly popular American and English detective novels and film noir genre. No one seemed prepared to admit that a glass of pastis—as it was diluted with water—contained less alcohol than a similar-size glass of wine.

Partly it was politics. Women had been given the right to vote in France after the country's Committee of National Liberation extended suffrage to women in 1944. Few politicians were prepared to legalize a drink that women still popularly equated with absinthe. Absinthe retained an image in most women's mind of dissolute men who came home inebriated to abuse their wives and children.

Paul never thought that women actually believed such nonsense; it was part of a misguided popular belief. Often politicians promised to resolve the situation, but once in office those promises were conveniently forgotten.

Paul garnered the support of the syndicate for drinks in Marseille, whose secretary, Louis Bergamaschi, was also an administrator for the Ricard distilleries.

The syndicate actively lobbied regional authorities with the argument that the clandestine pastis trade was dangerous for public health as it remained unregulated. Paul felt as if he were going back in time two decades when similar arguments helped legalize pastis in the 1930s. But despite their most strenuous efforts, their pleas still fell on deaf ears.

One of France's staunchest enemies was Germaine Poinso-Chapuis, a talented lawyer from Marseille who was the first woman to be appointed as a minister in a French government. She had played a pivotal role in the Resistance and, based on that reputation, had curried favor among many powerful politicians. In 1947, she was named head of the health ministry in the government of Robert Schuman and instituted a vociferous fight against alcoholism in France.

Paul felt her efforts misguided. Pastis could not be considered the only reason for alcoholism in France. Until the 1950s, wine was largely ignored as contributing to the problem of alcoholism, with spirits taking most of the blame. But, statistics showed that for every ten alcoholics, six were were addicted to wine and four to spirits.

Poinso-Chapuis was hated in Marseille. So much so that jokes about her became a means to palliate the simmering hatred for her attempts to slur pastis. Locals began to play on her name to *chapeau pointu*, or witch's hat. On one occasion the animosity boiled over. Poinso-Chapuis came to deliver an electoral speech in Sainte-Marthe, where Paul had based his pastis operations. When she took the podium, the throng applauded wildly; as soon as she opened her mouth to speak the atmosphere changed. The crowd hissed and launched vicious verbal attacks. She left without being able to finish her first sentence.

Robert Debré, a famous French doctor, in a study after the war, underlined that most alcoholism had its roots in social reasons and that waging war against the disease needed to begin from the ground up.

Paul would be preoccupied by the question of the morality of alcohol his entire life. He believed in much of Debré's analysis of alcoholism. Drink for him represented camaraderie and conviviality. That should not be forgotten. Paul drank in moderation. Alcohol was also an important agricultural and industrial product. Thousands of French people worked in the spirits industry. He did not understand efforts to demonize alcohol.

"Who can prove to us that people who drink water are more handsome, more intelligent, or more virtuous than wine drinkers, or that they are wittier and live longer?" Paul wrote on the subject. "The industry and commerce of wine and spirits have always been an essential activity for France."

The legalization of pastis seemed inevitable for Paul, who had been operating his factory semi-clandestinely. Locals knew it was only a matter of time until pastis would be legalized again. The government eventually would realize that it needed to collect taxes on the trade. Thumbing their noses at the law, many locals drank pastis in plain daylight on the café terraces of Marseille.

Paul came up with a brilliant idea. He knew that the government would have to bend soon and that the race to be atop the pastis pyramid would again hit full speed. He needed to get a head start on the competition. He dispatched Ricard representatives to bars and bistros to offer to reimburse any fines they were given for serving his pastis. The strategy paid huge dividends. Bar owners were more than happy to push Ricard before any other pastis drink. They need not worry about anything now. He also launched an anisette drink that was allowed under the current legislation since it was only 20 percent

Anisette Ricard Liqueur launched by Paul Ricard in the 1940s when the production and sale of 45% pastis was prohibited. This prohibition ended in 1951.

alcohol. He called it Ricard anisette. Now his name was circulating in the drinks trade again. He could even promote it.

Officially, however, the waiting game continued. Paul would allocate time to a luxury impossible to indulge in during war: travel.

He had long been fascinated by the United States. Even before the war he had admired from a distance what he considered American companies' considerable advance on Europe in certain manufacturing sectors, in particular distilling and packaging. One of his role models was Henry Ford, whom he idolized for his will to create unparalleled products and improve the treatment of his workers.

Ford had doubled his workers' wages to the famous $5 a day in 1913 and reduced their workday to eight hours. Ricard saw Ford's strategy as vital to good business practice. Many thought Ford was crazy for increasing his workers' wages. Yet it helped stabilize his workforce and decrease turnover. Meanwhile, workers thought they were getting a good deal. Ford wanted to help create a blue-collar middle class who could afford the products he sold. If people were richer, he would sell more, and in turn create more wealth for himself and others.

For Paul, Ford was an oracle. He already felt strongly about issues of social justice and equality. His pastis was a drink for everyone, no matter their socioeconomic category or class. But treating his workers well went beyond social justice. Its ulterior motive was a flourishing business. Paul was a paradox for many. While politically he aligned himself on the left in social policies, he espoused conservative fiscal policies. He did not like idealism. He had seen the ravages of it in war. Furthermore, the "cadre" class of functionaries that ran French politics seemed divorced from the reality a modern business had to face. Paul had ideals. But he was rooted in the real world and to finding solutions that fit each situation.

Later, Paul would urge his workers to buy their own houses. If they could not, he often provided the loans that allowed them to own property. This type of operation linked them indelibly to the company and spurred them to work even harder and more efficiently with the view to greater personal prosperity.

Like Ford, Paul seriously doubted that workers would contribute to the company enthusiastically if only for the reason it offered a paycheck. The link between company and worker—between the boss and the workers—had to run deeper. They had to feel as if they belonged to a family. Though this strategy is more prevalent today, it was revolutionary in postwar France. Paul was the first in France to offer his employees shares in the company to solidify their devotion to the common cause. It was a system that he had established in 1938 upon the death of his father. It wasn't purely symbolic.

Many of these beliefs were reinforced when Paul traveled to the United States in 1946.

Trip to the USA organized in 1946 by the French administration for selected entrepreneurs. First layover at Le Labrador (left).

Paul was excited to visit the U.S. for the first time. The trip was organized for several young French entrepreneurs in order to study work and production methods in the U.S. For Paul, it was also a valuable window into the mind of the U.S. consumer. He dreamed of taking his pastis to America and making a success there as well.

Paul kept a detailed journal of the trip, which started with a train trip from Marseille to Paris and, after several days waiting in the French capital, a long plane voyage that included a stop for refueling in Ireland before reaching New York, where he checked into the Commodore Hotel.

Paul was impressed by the immensity of the city. The hotel, with its 2,800 rooms, 28 floors and four bars, held particular sway over his imagination, as did the illuminated advertising panels on Broadway.

He had a long shower and sent a telegram to Marseille saying he had arrived safely. Everything was different in America. At the bar, most people drank beer or fruit juice, not wine or aperitifs as in France. When he tried a glass of California wine he understood why. It was a lot more expensive than beer and not very good.

Paul was astounded with the lifestyle of the American worker. Life was less expensive in America than in France, and workers made on average around $1.40 an hour more. Paul studied the situation in detail, laying out in a report delivered to Marseille's business leaders on his return, how many hours an American worker would need to work to buy everything from a gallon of gasoline to a house.

"When the French worker has earned enough to buy a suit, the American worker can buy a car," Paul said.

Paul visited an array of factories and businesses, from bread and cookie factories to Hershey's chocolate. He traveled to Detroit, where he visited the Ford plant and witnessed firsthand Henry Ford's massive complex that employed 72,000 workers and turned out 6,500 motors every 24 hours. Every hour, 60 cars were assembled on the long assembly line.

"Detroit is more agreeable than New York," observed Paul. "People are nicer and happier. Women are more flirty and elegant."

Paul hoped that he would be able to use the trip as a springboard to bringing his spirits to America. He saw plenty of opportunity to break into a market that was fractured and young, prohibition having been ended only at the beginning of the war.

Whiskey and gin were America's favorite spirits, which, Paul felt, left plenty of room for France's varied spirits to gain traction with American drinkers. He was prescient in his assessment that French brands needed to seduce American customers with prestige. He urged French companies already manufacturing their spirits in the U.S. to relocate production back in France and use the "Made in France" label as a moniker of quality and added value.

"We need to protect the prestige of our drinks," he said. "Our wine, liquor, and spirits should be of French origin."

At the same time, Paul wondered if American palates were sophisticated enough to enjoy the best France had to offer.

"American consumers aren't educated sufficiently in wines and are not yet ready to fully appreciate our finest wines more easily accessible and well priced. Consequently, our exports should be oriented toward quality wines."

What impressed Paul most was the absence of any animosity between the classes. The real boss was the client, not the "patron" who reigned over the French company. Even if the unions were very powerful, negotiations between workers and management were not guided by politics. Paul was amazed to see that a union leader and manager could stop to play golf or tennis between negotiations; the self-made man legend fascinated Paul.

It was not until May 1951 that the French government repealed the ban on the sale and manufacture of pastis at 45 percent alcohol. The day the law was formally repealed, the bells rang out triumphantly in Sainte-Marthe. The entire village came out to celebrate the fact that Ricard's factory would reopen its doors. A way of life was being revived.

Finally Ricard could come out of the shadows and operate legally.

In that same year, Paul opened a new 6,500-square-foot headquarters building in Sainte-Marthe to group all his needs to accommodate the rapid growth he predicted—and expected. Paul believed that bringing all of the company's various services and departments under one roof would help gain time and efficiency. The ground floor housed printing and photography services near the advertising and promotion staff, while the first floor held general management, the second floor head a meeting room and a screening room for films. Paul was proud to have created one of the most modern headquarters in France, replete with air conditioning (a rarity in France) and IBM office hardware. Paul gave the same sense of detail

Factory of Sainte Marthe, late 1950s.

and modernity to the bottling factory, contiguous to the offices. All operations, from distilling to labelling, were automated in 1951.

Sales exploded. In the first year, 1951, Ricard sold 10 million liters, a volume he doubled in a decade, reaching 20 million liters by 1961, and 30 million liters in 1965. By 1971, the company was selling 60 million liters of its pastis a year.

The postwar rebuilding years were a boon to French business. New buildings were erected and a new caste of middle-class workers strove to achieve comfort. Wages during this period rocketed by 15 percent, while at the same time prices grew at just under five percent. The French were discovering the *douceur de vivre* (the sweet life) as well.

Paid holidays of three weeks and more meant that more French workers were traveling than they had been in the past, particularly by automobile. It generated a feeling of freedom. The south and the warmer Provençal climate were among the most popular destinations. The famous French jazz singer Charles Trenet captured the national psyche in his popular song about the Route Nationale 7, which linked Paris to Menton by more than 600 miles of rambling *autoroute* via Burgundy, the Auvergne, the Rhône Valley, and finally the French Riviera. People were discovering the beautiful countryside outside of the cities and the fantastic sensation of cruising with what seemed to be not a care in the world.

The song's lyrics were evocative enough: "The summer sky fills our hearts with lucidity, chasing the blues and acidity that are the bore of our big cities...We're happy Nationale 7."

Ricard logo 1953.

Ricard logo 1958.

Ricard logo 1964.

LE VRAI PASTIS DE MARSEILLE

card logo 1984.

Ricard logo 1995.

Ricard logo 2010.

Advertisement for the "Cinq Volumes d'eau" campaign, 1960.

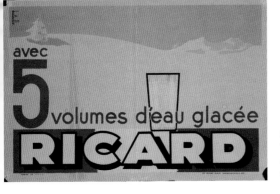

Seasonal variations of the "Cinq Volumes d'eau" campaign. From left to right and top to bottom: 1958, 1958, 1958, 1953, 1954.

Advertisement, 1957.

Le Garlaban 1964.

The Circuit Paul Ricard, 1970.

The Circuit Paul Ricard, 1970 (left). Paul Ricard at his namesake curcuit, 1980s.

Bendor Island.

Les Embiez Island.

Caslte of Sainte Marthe, Ricard family home, 2016 (photo Marc-André Desanges).

Trenet's song captured the democratization of the age and its hope for a brighter future. The Riviera was no longer just for rich Americans and the English. Now the French were on their way, too. The long road from Paris offered Paul a perfect theater to promote his product.

Even under the best conditions, the trip from Paris took two days. All along the road, Paul found plenty of space to promote his pastis on giant billboards. He had a captive audience who wanted nothing better than to arrive in the sunny climes to find a cold Ricard waiting to slake their thirst.

The postwar years came to be known as *Les Trente Glorieuses*— or "the thirty glorious years". Not only for the country as a whole, but also for Ricard. Paul felt that he was reliving his prewar success all over again.

Better pay across the entire social spectrum meant that more people had more disposable income. Not only were their pocketbooks fatter, but also the time they spent behind their desks was diminishing. More free time bred more hours to share a drink with a friend. Taking an aperitif was back on the social agenda. More pastis was being consumed to the detriment of other alcohol, including wine, whose annual consumption per capita fell from 162.5 liters in 1960 to 110 liters in 1970.

Ricard went on a hiring spree. The company grew from 442 people in 1951 to 1,084 in 1964 and 1,719 by 1967. Production multiplied by six during the same period that the number of employees increased four-fold.

Paul needed a new industrial model. His automated production line inevitably reduced the amount of manual workers that he employed, but meanwhile, he bolstered the number of sales representatives. Not only would this be vital for his expansion in France, but also abroad. Spain and Italy were among his first priories. For the latter, Paul created a specific Franco-Italian company, Anis, which was overseen by one of his trusted friends and lieutenants, who knew the ins and outs of the labyrinthine Italian market. The biggest overseas markets for Ricard were Algeria and Morocco, followed by Switzerland, Spain, Belgium, Tunisia, the then Belgian Congo, Greece, and Austria. By 1965, about 15 percent of the company's total sales were generated outside of France. Though modest, these numbers continued to grow yearly with Ricard pouring more and more energy into generating sales abroad.

Giving a seminar in the 1950s. Worldwide exportation strategy for Ricard teams by Paul Ricard.

Paul could no longer visit all of the clients and bars as he did in his youth. The company was too big and he was already spread thin performing his managerial duties. But Paul's early experience of being close to the customer would remain his mantra. He spent long hours studying regional results and tailoring his strategy to zones he believed could be more lucrative. Partly, this was achieved through advertising. But Paul also liked to build general hype around the Ricard brand.

As he began to open regional factories, he transformed those openings into events to bolster sales as well. He sought out visible locations, preferably one including an architectural landmark like a chateau, and he built state-of-the-art factories that he tried to make synonymous with a certain modern beauty. It had become vital to reduce transport costs with regional production facilities. After opening a factory in Bordeaux in 1952, he followed with a raft of others that included Lille in 1959, Thiais (outside of Paris) in 1962, Rennes in 1965, Dijon in 1966, and Lyon in 1968.

Paul's ideas for progress went far beyond building state-of-the-art factories. He commissioned projects for a "city" for his workers above Bandol, in the south of France, where they would have stores, sports facilities, a school, theaters, and gardens.

It was the first of many projects that Ricard would conceive of to take care of his employees. Paul believed that enriching his employees paved the path to success. He also felt the limitations of that scheme and wished to augment employees' loyalty to his cause with other socially-minded projects. Eventually it would lead to the building of full-blown vacation facilities that his employees used freely with their families, with only minimal charges for spouses. On-site he had Ricard restaurants and stores, where they could buy food and refreshments.

Paul believed that keeping his employees satisfied went well beyond the time spent at the office. But that counted equally. Each of his new facilities was conceived primarily with the well-being of his employees in mind. If they were not well looked after, efficiency would drop.

"Man spends the majority of his time at work. I've long dreamed of building offices and factories in a huge park surrounded by gardens, flowers, fountains, and statues," he said. "Man needs art and beauty... biologists have established that the setting, climate and atmosphere in which beings and plants live transform them completely. We believe that we should implement everything to elevate man and to make life better... In this world, where electronics free the spirit and the machine eases labor, a factory should no longer be hell, but become an earthly paradise, edified by art, that we will come to visit like a temple, or a cathedral. Industry that made man a slave at the end of the nineteenth century will be replaced by automation that will give him independence, liberty, comfort, and free time."

Paul was ready for his company to assume the global stature that it had achieved. Sales had exploded and net results soared. In 1961, he told a board meeting that the company could no longer shy from its ambitions. "Ricard is no longer just the pastis of Marseille or even just French pastis. It is a global drink and now it needs to be universal."

The preparations began for the company to join France's major industrial concerns. Ricard moved his headquarters to the French capital to a beautiful building on the Left Bank, at 2 rue de Solférino. He wanted a magnificent calling card to bolster the company's image.

The IPO in 1962 was a resounding success, with 352,000 shares floated at 50 francs a share. Ricard was valued at 17.6 million francs. Previously the company had been traded sparingly and solely on the Marseille Bourse. Even then, Ricard's stock had seen steady and fruitful gains.

Paris indeed propelled Ricard into more rarefied company. Between the first quarter of 1961 and 1962, the stock soared more than 100 percent. By 1964, the company's market value reached 350 million francs, and it exceeded 400 million francs in September 1965.

Ricard was on the national map. It was one of the incontestable leaders in its branch. Even the French state, with which Ricard had so many disputes, was beginning to pay attention. To wit: in 1966, a government commission invited Paul and his son Bernard to a working lunch in Paris to discuss the possibility that Paul head a group uniting France's agricultural concerns. Paul quickly dismissed the invitation as another attempt to shore up the government's bureaucratic reach. Uniting companies that made no profits made no sense. Certainly, he still resented having his personal finances subjected to examination a couple of years earlier. Paul responded to the government committee with an entreaty for them to reduce taxes and social charges in order to allow companies to do what they did best for the country: create wealth. He also told them that they should remand their stringent attacks against alcohol and let the sector operate with fewer restrictions.

Obviously, Paul and government were never made to coexist in harmony.

Maybe it was for that reason that when Charles de Gaulle came to visit Marseille in 1961, instead of accompanying all of his employees to catch a glimpse of the *grand homme*, Paul retreated into the empty Ricard offices in Sainte-Marthe. The General had declined to meet Paul. Ricard wasn't up the standards of de Gaulle's Republic. Ricard may have ranked among France's top taxpayers in terms of value, but it wasn't enough. The snub left Paul with a bad taste in his mouth.

Paul Ricard interpreting his own life in *No Pain, No Gain* while shooting the war and resistance scene, 1964.

Chapter Seven

IT WAS A BEAUTIFUL SUNNY DAY in June 1967 when Paul Ricard arrived in Cadaqués, on the Costa Brava in northern Spain. The light glimmered on the bay and the heat was dry and crisp. Paul liked Spain. Bullfighting was one of his passions. He owned a bullring at Méjanes, which he used to house a yearly festival in Camargue and where people dressed in traditional costume and watched the feria. In 1958, he even married his eldest daughter Danièle to a Venezuelan bullfighter, César Giron, in an elaborate wedding attended by such luminaries as Ava Gardner and Pablo Picasso. The mayor of Marseille performed the ceremony.

Paul made it a habit of traveling to Spain whenever he could, especially if Giron, whom some aficionados rank among the best *toreros* of the twentieth century, was fighting. His daughter lived with Giron in an apartment on the avenida Generalissimo Franco in the new part of Madrid. Like all toreadors, Giron had his ups and downs. As a young man he earned fame for dispatching bulls with considerable flair. In one fight, in the ancient walled town of Alcalá de Henares, he killed the bull and then ceremoniously cut off both ears. He presented the bloody prize to Ava Gardner. When the American star kissed one of the ears the arena broke into delirious applause.

Giron suffered his share of adversity in the ring, too. A bull gorged him in the thigh, barely missing his vital femoral artery, sending him to the hospital barely conscious. He had been trying to make a comeback, but it was proving difficult.

As he walked the streets of Cadaqués, Paul cleared his head. He was happy. He had come to meet the Spanish surrealist master Salvador Dali. Paul wanted to buy a watercolor from Dali that he would then use to make a print gift to his best clients at the end of the year. The idea of spending an afternoon with Dali was exciting.

Paul Ricard with Salvador Dali.

Although he appreciated Picasso, he revered Dali. Both were Spanish; the fact that the two greatest painters of his era hailed from the same country had not escaped Paul.

Paul felt the force in Picasso's pictures, but he understood Dali's art better. He gravitated to a more classical representation in painting, and Picasso's contorted cubist compositions did not always resonate with him. Dali's strange juxtapositions and haunting landscapes of the subconscious were curious, but his painting was impeccable. The lines and perspectives he employed were directly descended from classical painting. He subverted them into an entirely new vocabulary.

Paul, in the hundreds of paintings he had done, had mostly relied on classical techniques. He liked that when you looked at a picture, you could tell what it represented. When he did a portrait, you knew who the model was. The goal of his own art was to capture the personality of a person in a still picture, to show that person in an amplified reality. He considered himself an artist, but he was now meeting a master.

Dali's house in Port Lligat, just next to Cadaqués, was legendary. He had been painting and living in the small fishing village since 1930, when he bought a remote fisherman's *cabana* thanks to an advance from his patron, the famed collector, the Vicomte de Noailles, who with his wife Maire-Laure, had constituted one of the most important collections of art of the early part of the twentieth century.

Over the years, Dali expanded his property in measure with his success and, by the time Paul knocked on the door, lived in a rambling series of white cubes with an incredible view onto the bay below. For theatrical effect, Dali had placed a group of white swans in the bay where they floated languorously in the waves. Everything about Dali's home had been made to unsettle guests and show Dali in the most curious of lights. He wielded a cane and wore a wig.

Dali liked to receive guests from a throne—he aspired to an aristocratic life—but he showed deference to Paul and eagerly showed him around the studio, explaining some of the new techniques he had been employing in his work. The two men got along well. Recently Dali had been playing with moiré to achieve the impression of movement. The technique also had roots in the world of psychedelic drugs. Dali wanted to be a drug himself, he told Paul, who laughed at the maestro's eccentricities.

It was about this time that Paul was invited into Dali's main studio. As he entered, he froze in his tracks. The entire wall was covered with a monumental picture that Dali was in the midst of finishing.

Dali had been working on the picture for two years. It was a violent subject. In the center a baby, or maybe a cherub, is killing a huge tuna fish with a butcher's knife. All around, blood squirts from dying fish. Some are being gorged by mythological figures, others by ordinary fisherman. Some men looked like statues akin to Michelangelo's paintings in the Sistine Chapel. Smack in the bottom middle part of a canvas was a cartoonish man outlined in black and yellow in a Pop Art style. Dali told Paul that he wanted to mix all of the styles he had mastered in this one painting, from Surrealism to tachism to geometrical abstraction and psychedelic art. It would be his *chef d'oeuvre*. A masterpiece.

Paul was so transfixed by the picture that he could hardly follow Dali's explanations. Quickly he calculated in his head. He told Dali he would buy it when it was finished. Dali said it should be ready by the beginning of next year. The two men shook hands and repaired outside where they shared a drink in the shade from the warm sun.

The painting was a symbol of Paul's ambitions and aspirations. When it was delivered at his Paris headquarters, the press had amassed outside. It took a crane to lift the massive picture to the second-floor bay window. It was much too large to pass through the ground-floor door.

Once it was in place, Paul invited *le tout Paris* to come see it and to meet Dali, who received the crowds while seated on a huge armchair, cane in hand, mustache perfectly waxed, surrounded by a retinue that included his wife, Gala.

Paul loved the attention and the spectacle. So much so that he soon decided that he would send the painting on a national tour. Drumming up attention for Dali in this case would be garnering attention for Ricard. Paul never considered himself an art collector. In fact, this was the first important painting he had purchased. His other purchases were mostly limited to regional masters. But he soon realized that this picture could be a magnet for the type of attention that ultimately, he hoped, would help sell more pastis.

Dali's painting departed on its road show, first to Grenoble, where it arrived two days before the opening ceremonies of the 1968 Winter Olympics. Unfortunately, Paul hadn't measured the size of the entrance to the hall where it was destined to be hung: the painting's size kept it from passing through the door. He hurriedly found an alternative at a school of fine arts.

By the end of its travels, the painting had gained a special aura, not only for its majestic size, but also its powerful subject. Paul decided to hang it like a crown jewel in a gallery that he constructed on the island of Bendor. A woman named Mireille welcomed visitors in the daytime and a watchman guarded the painting in the evening. Around the painting he hung a selection of minor pictures that he changed every couple of months in order to invite people to the gallery.

Paul expected the painting never to move again. Yet it didn't take long for the painting to become a cause célèbre for another reason. In a daring raid, thieves one evening circumvented the security and cut the painting from its support. They rolled it up and made off with their loot.

The morning after the crime brought pandemonium. All of Paul's assistants were frantic. Geneviève Latour, his personal secretary, found Paul inspecting a sailing boat that morning. Even before she arrived, she cried at the top of her lungs. "The Dali has been stolen! It's been stolen..."

She was astonished when Paul looked up from what he was doing with complete tranquility. "Have you called the police and notified the press?" he asked.

"We have to call the reporters, the radio, and the television," he instructed. "Then the police and customs so they can't get it out of the country."

While everyone else was frantic, Paul remained calm. He knew that the situation was beyond his control. Just as it had in his possession, the painting would now garner attention in its disappearance. The press was full of reports of the painting's disappearance. Ricard was in the headlines again.

It would take another decade before the painting reappeared. It was found hidden in a luggage deposit in a train station. After extensive restorations, the painting was remounted on its frame and installed in the reception rooms at the Ricard headquarters in Sainte-Marthe.

Paul had a flair for the theatrical. Everything he did had the ulterior motive of generating attention for his brand. He realized relatively quickly how impactful it could be to associate his brand with films, events, and even sports. In some ways his decision to do so was dictated by necessity—a law was passed in France in 1951 forbidding print and poster advertisements for all anise-based drinks. In addition, associating his name with a larger-than-life event perfectly suited his desire for attention.

He formed an in-house advertising office that worked furiously on ideas to promote the brand within the growing limitations of the law. Perhaps the most successful effort was Ricard's hitching on to the ultimate French sporting event, the Tour de France bicycle race. Its more than 3,000 miles of racing, spread over a month of competition, was just the kind of drawn-out event that suited Paul's appetite for theatrics. He outfitted a truck like a boat with Ricard blue-and-yellow masts that followed the tour and, in the evening, transformed into a Ricard "pavilion." All along the way, the truck distributed Ricard hats

Ricard Caravel at the Tour de France, 1952.

and other paraphernalia to spectators, turning the crowds massed along the side of the road into a moving ad for Paul's brand.

After each stage, Paul pitched a music hall where he brought his favorite singers to perform songs evocative of the sun and ambience of Provence and Marseille. An accordionist belted out folk tunes that kept people dancing all night long. All the while they sipped Ricard.

The success of Paul's efforts on the Tour spurred him on to other, more innovative adventures. The Tour only happened once a year, and it was important to permeate the consumer psyche. Paul thought that he needed to approach his audience where it would be receptive. He hired an old buddy who specialized in photographic journalism to scour the beaches during the summer months to snap pictures of vacationers.

In the evening, Ricard set up an enormous screen and projected the pictures of that day in a giant slideshow. Of course it all came outfitted with Ricard paraphernalia. The success exceeded expectations. People massed around in the hope of spotting themselves on the beach, having fun. The Ricard name seeped into their psyche. Consumers were unconsciously equating Ricard with the best of times.

A multitude of like-minded projects was carried out with varying degrees of success. One of Paul's more far-flung publicity stunts even included mounting a float in support of the secession of Montmartre from the rest of Paris. It was all done in the spirit of fun. And it resulted in a great party—thanks to Ricard.

When the Suez crisis erupted in 1956 and the gas pumps began to run dry, Paul came up with a scheme to bring "relief" to the people of Paris. If his delivery trucks were incapable of bringing his aperitif to cafés, he needed to find an alternative. Brainstorming, he began to think about the Sahara, the desert, thirst, and...camels.

Delivery of bottles via camels when the Suez Canal was closed in 1956.

Why shouldn't he hire a herd of camels to help deliver his drinks to Paris cafés? It would be the "crusade against thirst." He immediately hired a herd of dromedaries outfitted with camel jockeys in full blue-and-yellow Ricard regalia to deliver his drinks to cafés along the Champs-Élysées and elsewhere across Paris.

People stopped dead in their tracks in disbelief. Children hurled cries of joy. Newspapers, radio, and television talked constantly of the dromedaries around town delivering the Marseille pastis. The success was complete.

With every event Paul found more and more unusual ways of grandiose promotion. The more improbable or far-fetched, the better suited they were to grab attention.

One day, as a bet, he organized a trip for forty to Italy. What at first seemed crazy turned into a caravan of Ricard cars moving slowly across Europe. No promotion was in vain. Each following year he organized similar trips to Belgium, Spain, and Luxembourg, to name but a few. On one such expedition a convoy of 80 blue-and-yellow Ricard cars took people across Europe.

During the winter of 1959 Paul rented out a number of luxury hotels across the French Riviera as part of a huge party. Another time he took 530 passengers with him on a boat trip to visit the twelfth-century Koutoubia mosque in Marrakesh, Morocco. Along the way, high-profile calls were made at the ports of Bastia and Ajaccio in Corsica.

Paul's appetite for promotion could not be satiated. When Pope John XXIII acceded to the papacy in 1958, Paul hit on the idea to

Papal audience with Juan XXIII on a trip to Rome with employees of Ricard Society, 1961. Paul Ricard offers a gift to the pope.

travel to Rome with his workers to pay homage to the newly elected pontiff. In 1948, the not-yet pope had visited Paul on his farm in Camargue. Paul felt a special link to His Holiness for that reason.

The trip hardly escaped notice. Paul hired trains that were painted in the Ricard colors to transport 1,200 people on the voyage. Inside the carriage there were horses from Camargue and a white lamb that he would present to the pontiff. It was over the top and Paul liked it that way.

Nothing went without notice. Even his person. At times he would be seized by terrific fits of rage. Although he demanded perfection from his workers—as he demanded it from himself—his unpleasantness was calculated for maximum effect. Just like a good military leader, he knew the importance of respect from his troops. And as disturbing as these fits could appear, Paul never crossed the border into vulgarity. He would yell and throw plates and glasses. Part of his rage, of course, was sincere. Nothing went fast enough for him. During these moments, his employees knew better to say nothing. They knew that it was in these moments that Paul, who grew frustrated with any resistance to his plans, was blowing off the steam that had accumulated inside of his brain as the gears turned inside to formulate new plans.

For Paul, the nemesis to progress was the French administration. It appeared to him that the government was more intent on finding ways of hindering growth than on fostering it.

In January 1962, when Paul introduced his company to the stock exchange, he had already been distributing shares to employees for years. He reckoned that incentivizing employees was the best way to increase production. Everyone across all pay grades were concerned. Many took the shares in the company without further consideration; to them, it was just another piece of paper. Paul already motivated them with his generous salary scheme and the family-like organization he favored.

A month after Ricard went public, Modeste Bovis, Paul's cleaning lady whose father and husband had also worked for Ricard, asked for an appointment with Monsieur Ricard, who received her in his office.

Paul and Modeste had known each other since youth. She had her first communion the same day as Paul, they had gone to school together, and Modeste's father had worked for Paul's father. The day she was married, her husband came to work at Ricard.

Understandably, Paul and Modeste were on friendly terms. She addressed Paul with the informal "tu," and she took the liberty to dispense sisterly-like admonitions, such as he wasn't eating or sleeping enough. She even went so far as to tell him he wasn't dressed well enough for a man of his station.

She had a mysterious air as she waited, finally complaining to one of Paul's secretaries that she had been deeply unlucky in life.

When Paul met her face to face, she said, "I need to ask you something."

"Go ahead, Modeste," entreated Paul.

"You know, I have a lot of stock in the company. I have mine, and my poor father's and my late husband's. I kept them all, as you told us to."

Indeed, Paul had always told his employees that their stocks would one day appreciate. Many had listened religiously to his recommendations. Others had sold at the first opportunity, to buy a car or get money for a vacation.

"Last night," continued Modeste, "I invited friends over to drink a Ricard. And they told me that I was a millionaire. I thought they were making fun of me at first. But not at all. They explained that the stock that I had was worth a thousand times more than before Ricard was listed on the bourse de Paris. I couldn't sleep a wink. I couldn't stop doing the sums in my head and it all seemed impossible. I needed to see you and make sure that it was true. That it's not all a joke."

A smile came across Paul's face as he listened to Modeste. He was particularly pleased with the idea that his cleaning lady was coming to the realization that she was now one of the richest people that she knew.

"Well, Modeste," said Paul. "You should be rich, like all the other old employees of the company. I promised you as much. How many shares do you have?"

She responded with a high number and Paul did the math surreptitiously in his head.

"You're fifty times a millionaire," said Paul.

At this point, Modeste sat down on the nearest chair. It looked as if she would faint. She was stunned and silent.

"When I distributed the shares," continued Paul, "you didn't believe that one day you would all be capitalists with cars and houses. Are you convinced now?"

Modeste nodded enthusiastically. It looked as if she would cry for joy.

"Now that I have so much money," she said suddenly, "I hope you won't be upset that I stop doing the cleaning."

"Of course not," said Paul. "It's time that you enjoyed life."

Modeste all the same continued cleaning the house for the few days that it took to find a replacement. She bought herself an astrakhan coat and a gold bracelet. Every year she sent Paul a postcard from one of the exotic locations that she visited during an extravagant cruise.

One afternoon Paul was working in the garden on the island of Bendor. He had bought the island in 1950 when he learned it was for sale. Located only a few hundred yards from the coast and the village of Bandol, the island was a rocky, forgotten wasteland. But it had piqued Paul's imagination for as long as he could remember. Living on an island was highly attractive to him. Isolation and silence were the things he cherished most. He needed them to think and work. Although he liked people, he had a pronounced need for solitude. His first idea had been to build a residence for him and his family. But his need for isolation caved in favor of his need to create something bigger. Soon he was formulating plans to build a series of houses for friends on the island. Not long after, the idea had evolved: he would put up a hotel. It would all look very Provençal, with the houses pink and pastel hues of green. As soon as building began, Paul added an art gallery, a glass-blowing atelier, a museum of the sea, a theater, bars, and restaurants. Paul was on a roll.

Paul Ricard purchased Bendor Island in 1950 and completed development in 1970.

Creating from scratch always got Paul's juices flowing. An unpopulated island with no buildings was an Eden waiting for a prime mover to give it life. As Paul's projects took form on the island, another nearby island, not 15 minutes away by motorboat, came up for sale. He bought it in 1958.

Whereas the island of Bendor was a small jewel, his newest island, Les Embiez, was a much larger rock in the sea, affording him many more possibilities. This time, he had no illusions of solitude. He wanted to transform Les Embiez, a short ten-minute ferry ride to the town of Six-Fours-les-Plages, into a buzzing tourist hub with an important hotel and a world-class port. The latter he started digging as soon as the deed was signed. Paul wanted a port not only fit for the boats of others, but he also wanted a port where he could moor his own schooner. Les Embiez provided Paul with a much larger palette.

Paul Ricard purchased Les Embiez Island in 1958 and completed development in 1995.

There was even a small vineyard that made rosé wine. He wanted to preserve much of the natural characteristics of the island, with its pine trees and rugged terrain. He liked to brag that almost the entirety of the regional flora was represented on his island alone.

Nearest the mainland, the island forms a U shape. The part that faces toward the open sea is mountainous with wild scrub and dramatic cliffs. Paul enjoyed long walks on the meandering paths he traced around the island, contemplating the ocean below. He thought that he would like to be buried there, looking out to sea (which he ultimately was). The island was shaped by the wind. Even the pine trees sloped close to the ground, formed by the constant blowing off the sea.

Gardening gave Paul time to think. He never minded getting his hands dirty. He found watching plants grow to be particularly satisfying. Although Paul was happiest zipping from one project to the next, he needed occasional moments of peace.

As he was watering the garden one Sunday, a man accosted Paul and, without realizing who he was addressing, demanded to see Paul Ricard.

"I don't think he's on the island," replied Paul, who was wearing a blue-and-white-checked worker's apron.

"What!" exclaimed the man. "A sailor told me he was here. Go on, son, tell me where I can find him."

"Ah," continued Paul, amused at the game. "I haven't the slightest idea. You can't talk to Monsieur Ricard just like that. You need to set an appointment with his secretary. And she doesn't work on Sundays.

You should write."

"Write! Do you have any idea who I am?"

The man was red in the face with rage.

"Monsieur Ricard knows me. I'm his friend. He's proud to shake my hand. If you keep me from seeing him—watch out! I'll have your job!"

With that the man turned on his heel and stormed off.

Paul liked what success had brought him—the means to realize projects—but the trappings of fame had little appeal. He hated everything obsequious and pretentious. He much preferred people with simple values. The no-nonsense decoration of his home and office pointed to this preference. Possessions attached little importance to him. He liked having the tools for work, like the dozens of Montblanc fountain pens he kept. But everything desirable was useful for Paul: a tool for living, a place to sleep, eat, and work. Or, to work, sleep, and eat in that order. Nothing was extravagant in his manner of living. Even for dinner he was most happy with a piece of cheese and a little salami.

One February afternoon he walked into the snack bar on Les Embiez just as two Englishmen were asking for a steak. It was the dead of winter, cold and windy outside. Only the pastry chef was in, and when the waitress told him what the clients wanted he refused. "I don't make steak," he protested.

He didn't consider it his job.

Paul happened in on the scene as it unfolded. Never did he hesitate to take matters into his own hands. Without a word, he hopped behind the bar and into the kitchen. He cooked the steaks himself, set the table, and even offered the two Englishmen a free aperitif.

He never said a word of reproach to the pastry chef. But as Paul left the island later that day, the chef had been given his walking orders. Paul demanded everything from his employees. If they didn't deliver—no matter at what level of company hierarchy—they did not belong.

One day he ordered a meeting of all his managers. They assembled with a certain trepidation, not knowing what the boss had in mind. Paul arrived in high spirits and shook everyone's hand, engaging in some small talk. Then he got to the crux of the meeting. On the island of Bendor there was a young man who worked at the most menial jobs. He cleaned up and fixed whatever needed repairing. He wasn't the brightest of kids, but he never complained in his work. He got coffee for people and delivered mail.

The other day, Paul had seen the young man sweeping up. The only problem was that it was windy and that he was sweeping against the wind. His work was in vain. Paul told the young man's manager that he had to explain to the lad how he should do his job so as not to waste time.

The managers Paul had summoned had passed by similar problems every day but were too busy with their own schedules to pay attention to the details. If you don't see every detail in your job, you can't do it properly. Paul Ricard believed that everything was important. You can't ignore such a thing.

Things did not always go as one planned however.

Paul loved to fly in his helicopter over the rugged hills above Bandol. The view was incredible and he could see exactly how he wanted his lands to develop. Yet one day, as he was flying above the Castellet, where he had built an airport, the helicopter crashed to the ground. He and his son Patrick were inside. Patrick walked away from the wreckage with hardly a scratch. Paul broke his jaw. Six months were needed for it to heal. Six months in which he could hardly speak and was relegated to communicating through written messages. It was a time of reflection for Paul. He would never fly a helicopter again.

Trip to Rome with the staff of the Ricard Society, 1961.

Chapter Eight

PAUL HAD BUILT SUCCESS ON HIS OWN TERMS, having negotiated some of the most trying times of the twentieth century, including global political meltdown, financial depression, and war. Even in the midst of prodigious adversity, he had shown that the human spirit could overcome great hardship with determination and creativity. He had little stomach for being told what to do. Although Ricard was one of the most prosperous companies in postwar France, Paul felt that with every year the administrative red tape, taxes, and charges were weighing on his patience. He could not fathom how a government could stack the cards so high against business. He himself felt that he was working in the best interest of France and that his company, in creating jobs and wealth, contributed to the image of the country as a whole. He had been working for four decades, building every day.

Perhaps the most satisfying project presently was his islands. He had even built an office there. Working on the island was a way of retreating into the tranquility he required to think. Over the years he had noticed that noise drowned out so much of what was best in men. One needed to tune into one's own inner voice. That impetus of self kept one marching to one's own drum. Success was a matter of conviction.

With the help of his secretary, Geneviève Latour, Paul got through his work rapidly and then retreated into his cherished moments of reflection and solitude. There were masses of papers and correspondence to be dealt with. All types of people wrote to Paul, even students.

He always took time to respond to their letters and was particularly happy to dispense advice on how best to succeed. He liked telling the story of his early years and how he had seen the world change into the quick-paced landscape of the second half of the twentieth century, where travel across continents was becoming relatively simple and computers and automated production lines had relieved man from the most strenuous labor.

"Humbly and sincerely, I work to achieve beauty, to paint as well as possible. Perfection, as Salvador Dali told me one day, is impossible!" he wrote in response to one schoolgirl who had asked Paul questions about his life.

Paul spent hours organizing his papers with Latour. There were reams and reams of archives. He never threw anything away. He kept clippings from the press, some that had nothing to do with the company, and filed them away for future consultation. Most were merely buried in a cemetery of paper, much of which still exists today.

During those days in November 1968, few if any of Paul's closest associates or family realized what was going on in his head. None could have imagined that he was preparing to make a decision that would leave many in his entourage flabbergasted in its scope and finality.

On November 15, 1968, he invited a journalist from the French national newsweekly *Match* for an interview. In the week leading up to the interview, Paul appeared distracted and uncommonly secretive. He asked for copies of documents, including the copy of a letter he had dispatched to the French Prime Minister protesting a law coming up for vote that would levy further taxes against alcohol.

Paul had had enough of taxes. It felt as if the government was doing everything in their power to prevent him—and other business leaders like him—from doing what they did best: create.

When the reporter arrived at Bendor, Paul received him alone. A few hours later, he called for his secretary, who arrived to find a scene that she little expected. The reporter was anxious. Paul had just dropped a bomb: he was planning to resign from the company he had dedicated his life to constructing. He was about to leave Ricard.

No one could believe the news.

Even the reporter kept asking Paul if it was really true, whether they could really publish. It made little sense to those around Paul. Why would one of France's most accomplished businessmen, a man decorated with respect and wealth, resign at the top of his glory? Ricard the company was growing more successful every day and it appeared that little would keep it from reaching even greater achievements.

What was the boss up to?

Some of his collaborators thought that he was trying to make a very public protest against the state of affairs in France and a government that he thought staunchly anti-business. Paul threatened to turn the company over to the French government to see if they could run it. It was pure bluff. But somewhere deep inside of him, Paul wanted to push the government through what he thought would be a public protest against their inefficiency.

Whatever his reasons, it became painfully clear that he meant business.

The next morning, on Saturday, he was in his office working with his secretary on the resignation letter he planned to send to the press when his son Patrick phoned.

Paul had made his decision without sharing his intentions with a soul, even his family. Patrick was stunned.

"Papa," he entreated Paul. "This is our family business. You can't just get up and leave. You brought us up with the responsibility of making it prosper. You raised us in the cult of work, that one day we would take over from you. It's your company. It's all of our company. You can't leave us. You just can't."

Paul told Patrick that it was his decision and that it was final.

"You can't tell me what to do," responded Paul. "I'm the boss. It's my decision. I'm not waiting on my children to give me any advice."

With that, he told Patrick that he would see him at the news conference he was organizing on Monday to publicly announce his departure.

That Monday morning felt to many at Ricard like a funeral. Employees could not even watch the conference if they wanted to. So many reporters had packed into the salons at the chateau in Saint-

Marthe that there was no additional standing room. The employees milled around outside, moping.

Bernard Ricard did not come. Of Paul's children, only Patrick and Danièle attended.

Patrick paced back and forth. He kept mumbling that it was impossible that his father would really carry out his threat. He could not abandon the firm he had created. Paul was resolved in his choice. After the news conference, he spent a couple hours on the Radio Monte Carlo explaining his decision as listeners called in to ask questions.

"There is one thing I can no longer stand," he said on the radio. "That is the constraints, the constraints of a technocratic system that, I believe, are outdated and not adapted to the world today... On the contrary, the system is engineered to bridle, to break, and even for certain industries, such as mine, to persecute and to complicate life for business leaders. In one word, they want to stop expansion, the expansion of free enterprise. I ask myself where they intend to go... If they want private enterprise to disappear, they should say it publicly."

Later that same afternoon, Paul stood in front of his staff to deliver a speech.

Paul was wound up. Already he had strayed from his scripted speech to the reporters, venturing into all manner of subjects, but particularly the government and how it was aligned against business. As he spoke to his staff he lamented the government's lack of efficiency in all matters, from not building enough schools to not building good roads and not bolstering telephone lines to improve communications. If citizens were paying so many taxes, shouldn't there be something to show for it?

He offered a laundry list of his gripes.

"It is intolerable that an administration that was created to serve the nation today wants to put that nation at its service and its orders," complained Paul. "It is prosperous companies that contribute to the greatness and prestige of this country. It is these companies that keep the state alive."

He continued, "Running a company is a great responsibility, one cannot improvise, take just any decision. It is governing. It is planning...."

"The future is the truth of tomorrow and not that of yesterday. Truth is the evolution of our past results. To refuse progress is all too easy, but it is also to refuse the combat of life, to prefer the status quo, death, nothingness, forever."

Paul concluded: "Over the last 40 years I certainly made my share of mistakes. I swear to you that they were involuntary, since I've always hoped to do a good job. If I didn't succeed, I wasn't meant to succeed.

"Also, it is with a clear conscience—since I never felt any ill will against those that voluntarily caused me hardship—that I cast an eye from time to time to the past.

"I've been lucky to live in one of the most interesting times in history.

"Thinking to the future, to the world of tomorrow, I am convinced that other younger people, better prepared for this new life, should enter the fray to trace their path.

That is how life is. Men pass like the days."

When Paul stepped back from the podium, his employees erupted in applause. It was a curious reaction. One that Paul was not entirely prepared for. Perhaps he wanted to see how far he could go. Perhaps he wanted to push the government into a corner. In fact, it was he who found himself in a corner.

His employees always applauded Paul's allocutions.

Maybe, if they hadn't done what they always did, but instead had protested and tried to dissuade him with their entreaties, Paul would have renounced his plan to step away from his duties. Perhaps that was the endgame. Perhaps he got caught in his own game as some of his closest collaborators believed.

"I could see that Paul didn't entirely expect their reaction," said Geneviève Latour. "The staff could probably have convinced him to change his mind at that moment. But no one did. The die is cast."

Was it by chance that very shortly after his resignation he fell ill? Doctors couldn't tell him what he had. He had pain all up and down his arms and in his shoulders. It was one of those illnesses for which there is really no cure. Was it his body responding to emotional shock? Paul was convinced that illness was caused by the dampness near the sea. He decided to move off the island to the wild scrubland above Bandol between Castellet and Signes, where he owned some 600 acres of craggy land. It was picturesque and remote. If a hermit had been looking for a place to retreat into solitude, this was it.

There was a small stone shepherd's house on the property. All around were wild low-lying trees and bushes and jagged rocks. From the top of the mountain you could see the entire coast spread out below from La Ciotat to Bandol and beyond. His two islands floated in the blue sea.

In the evening Paul looked up at the stars, trying to remember the constellations he had learned in his youth. He no longer felt that he was hurried. There wasn't even a telephone on the premises. During the day he painted, then fell fast asleep as soon he went to bed. He wanted to live like a pauper. He decided that he would make goat cheese. It was not long before the pain in his body dissipated, which his doctor attributed to him living at a higher altitude in the hills.

Living simply in self-imposed solitude gave Paul plenty of time to rehash all of his recent decisions. He reasoned his resignation to himself by convincing himself that he was exhausted. Over the last four decades he had hardly taken any time for himself. He had no time for the theater, to go to museums, or even to spend time with his family. Everything had been work. Physically he felt exhausted. He had had no time to recharge the batteries. Every trip—and they had been frequent—had been work-related.

With time, also, Paul had grown more frustrated with administrative roadblocks to his projects and less inclined to hold his tongue. A leader of a company such as his may need to be more politically restrained.

His recent helicopter accident had been a stark brush with death. It was closer than he had ever come before. It had made him realize that he was not immortal and that he needed to think not only about the future of others, but he also needed to consider his own future.

What would happen to the firm he had labored so hard to create once he was dead? If he had died then, the company would undoubtedly be embroiled in a difficult succession situation. His children certainly would have been faced with heavy estate taxes. It would have been an enormous load for the company to bear. Would the company have even survived his death at that time?

Paul thought that he had made Ricard too much in his image. It was time to ease off the reins and let someone else run around the world promoting the brand.

"When one has responsibilities," he thought, "one hasn't the right to die without preparing one's death."

It wasn't certain, however, that even Paul ascertained fully all of the reasons he had done what he had done. Of course, all of his explanations were logical, but there was something inside of him that had pushed him into a decision that defied logic. Maybe it was merely that his freedom felt impinged. Paul had a vital need for freedom in order to live.

In the days after his retirement, Paul continued to work, alone with his secretary, without any great urgency. His son Bernard, whom Paul had appointed his successor, had taken over his job at Ricard. It was now his ship to navigate.

Bernard's style and vision diverged from Paul's. The press lauded him for being a "calmer" version of his father, with a head for taking Ricard into new markets and acquisitions. Paul no longer sat on the board, but he was a definite éminence grise looking over his son's shoulder. He wrote him many letters, offering advice and telling him

Patrick, Bernard, and Paul Ricard.

how proud he was of his achievements.

In 1969, the company continued its ascent, selling 46 million bottles. In 1971, the company sold 60 million bottles.

Although business seemed to be strong, stress points had begun to show between Paul and Bernard. Paul had always taken on his diversification projects through new divisions of the company, whether the islands for tourism or his many real estate investments. Bernard wanted to steer the company slowly from its core product of pastis and diversify more into what he saw as the promising markets of wine and champagne.

Bernard wanted to assert his personality. He wanted to be different from his father. Whereas Paul was accessible, Bernard was distant. Much of it was just a difference in personality due to Bernard's timid disposition. Nonetheless, Bernard and Paul's relationship began to fray. Although Paul tried not to meddle in his son's business—he had abdicated the throne—it proved impossible. The company bore his name. It was his creation.

In a letter Paul addressed to Bernard in 1970, he laid bare some of his growing concerns.

"I left not to come back," he wrote to his son. "For 20 years I prepared my successor as one prepares a prince to become king.

"Certain people on the outside think that for some time I've continued to pull the strings.

"On the inside, I've been blamed for leaving and not wanting to help my son.

"I've told everyone that I am no longer needed, that I put in place everything needed to continue my work, to respect my ideas and principles."

Paul continued to elucidate how some of the employees at Sainte-Marthe deplored the lack of communication that Bernard had offered since his arrival. "The personnel would like to know why information has stopped circulating in the company. What are the reasons that dialogue has been cut between the directors and the managers and the worker's union? The old principles on which the company found success may be outdated but what has replaced them?"

"I remain at the disposal of the board of directors to give them my suggestions and offer my counsel... To have an open dialogue is not only to explain but to listen to others. It is by listening to others that we understand what they think, what they know and what they want...

"Life is made such that it awards pain and effort. Modesty is a virtue because it allows us to be corrected by our subordinates in order to avoid committing faults publicly. Be modest and audacious as much as possible and you will triumph. It is your victory that I wish."

Paul signed with love.

A year later the already difficult situation between father and son went south. Paul thought that Bernard left unheeded his recommendations and that he was acting without the best interests of the company at heart. The last straw came with Bernard's decision to secure a large loan in order to acquire the Lanson champagne brand.

In one respect, one could hardly blame Bernard. He had inherited his father's panache for sudden decisions. He wanted to grow the company as he saw fit. He wanted complete independence, free of his father's influence. When Paul opened the morning paper to read the news, he was furious. Paul was incensed that Bernard had secured 60 million francs in bank loans to cover the acquisition. One of his holy mantras was not to turn to banks, which he considered fair-weather friends. When things went bad they never had the vision to understand one's long-term goals and potential.

And then, Bernard had only purchased 48 percent of Lanson. What good would that do?

The relationship between father and son had reached a breaking point. In October 1971, Bernard handed in his resignation. Working under the shadow of his father proved too much for him to handle.

It underscored the extent to which Paul demanded much more from his family than sometimes they were willing to give. The relationship between an eldest son and a father can prove difficult. It would be less tumultuous when his second son Patrick took the reins a few years later.

Meantime, the company was to be run in the interim by one of Paul's cousins. The rift between father and son had exposed the company to its main rival, Pernod. Bernard had sold some of his shares to Pernod in the belief that the two companies needed to bond in order to fight together the battle for pastis against the growing market from American whiskey and other spirits. Paul himself had already sold some of his shares to Pernod in a controversial move to shore up finances for the projects he wanted to pursue in his retirement, in particular the construction of a world-class Formula One racetrack in Castellet.

When Paul presented the plan to the board of directors at Ricard to get financing for his track, they had rejected the plan as too costly. Paul was bitter to think that Bernard and the others he had given so much to were aligned against him.

It was then that he turned to Pernod. For his old employees, who all of their working life had demonized Pernod as the evil competition, the move was incomprehensible. They had a hard time swallowing the explanation that times were no longer the same and that Pernod was no longer the *diable*. Paul had grown to believe that the future resided in building an alliance with Pernod in order to fortify Ricard's position. The pastis trade faced numerous hurdles. American and British

Paul Ricard and Jean Hemard signing for PERNOD RICARD merger, 1975.

firms were swooping up market share with their whiskey and scotch. The fate of Ricard and Pernod was sealed in 1974. The two former rivals had come with a peace treaty between the two great figures of the pastis trade of the twentieth century, Paul Ricard and Jean Hémard. At the time of the signing, Ricard represented 45 percent of the French pastis market, while Pernod held 25 percent. Together they sold 100 million bottles a year and accounted for 55 percent of all French aperitif trade. The deal was carefully crafted so as not to weaken the two separate entities but to strengthen them against growing competition. Pernod brought with it its expertise in international distribution, while Ricard brought its stellar sales record. The two united into a holding company that made it the foremost European drinks group.

Both companies realized that the landscape they had helped

define was changing diametrically. The drinks business was becoming global, and organic growth would soon give way to a rash of mergers and acquisitions that initiated a race among groups to assemble the best brands.

Bernard Ricard had undoubtedly held similar beliefs. But it was perhaps easier for his brother Patrick to finally implement many of those changes when he assumed the presidency of the new behemoth in 1978. He quickly set the objective of diversification and growing his business through international expansion. He wanted to realize 50 percent of his business internationally. At the time that he acceded to the throne, less than 20 percent of business was international.

In 1975, the group had the equivalent of 430 million euros in sales, with a workforce of 6,500. By 1988, sales had grown to 2.05 billion euros with 11,000 workers, while in 1998 sales hit 3.14 billion. In 2008, sales hit a whopping 7 billion with nearly 20,000 employees.

Paul had been a visionary, but Patrick took the company to the next level with his own innovative strategy. Late in his career, people would describe his success as having taken a "small" family firm and turned it into a global behemoth. He began with a series of acquisitions that started with the purchase of America's Austin Nichols almost as soon as he arrived at the helm. It offered the foothold in the vital American market that his father had struggled to achieve. With the Wild Turkey brand, Austin Nichols was a chance too good to pass up. Patrick knew growth was tantamout to success, and in his drive to expand Ricard he surrounded himself with able lieutenants like Thierry Jacquillat and Pierre Pringuet, who would eventually succeed Patrick at the the head of the firm following his untimely death.

Times indeed had changed. Paul did not like to rely on debt to facilitate growth, but the purchase of Austin Nichols would cost 100 million dollars. Yet there was little hesitation from Patrick. The deal brought with it new prestige on the stock market as well as recognition of the group's international ambitions. A string of high-profile acquisitions followed, including the Irish Distillers whiskey portfolio and Havana Club rum. He stepped on the accelerator with the purchase of part of America's Seagram, which held such brands as Chivas Regal, The Glenlivet and Royal Salute scotch whiskies, and Martell cognac, followed by Britain's Allied Domecq, with brands such as Beefeater gin, Kahlua and Malibu liqueurs, Mumm and Perrier-Jouët champagnes, and Ballantine's whisky. The resulting company was a true giant. It now had a stable of covetable brands. One of the crowning achievements of this aggressive strategy was the takeover in 2008 of Vin&Spirit, the owner of the renowned Absolut vodka brand.

If there was one thing Patrick had taken from his father, it was audacity. Paul felt complete and total admiration for his son. Patrick may have done it differently than papa, but Paul had done it differently than his father before him, too.

Now Patrick boasted a company with brands of impressive pedigree. Historical brands appealed greatly to his love of provenance and time-tested quality. Many of the new brands dated to the early- to mid-1800's. Chivas, for example, was founded in the mid-nineteenth century by two brothers from Aberdeen, Scotland, who pioneered

Paul with his son, Patrick.

the whisky blending approach to craft a unique house taste, and then went on to position their whisky innovatively on the luxury market with a sophisticated mixture that they called Chivas Regal. It quickly exploded into an international phenomenon.

Another of his whisky houses, The Glenlivet, was founded even earlier, in 1824, as the first licensed distillery in the Livet valley of Scotland. The whisky's fame accrued to the extent that it was trademarked as The Glenlivet in 1884 to solidify its identity and to separate it from imitators trying to ride on the coattails of its success.

Perhaps, however, Patrick felt particularly proud of his acquisition of Absolut vodka. It was a brand recognized not only for its innovative marketing strategy, but also for its long history of excellence. Founded in the 1860s by a renegade Swedish entrepreneur, Lars Olsson Smith, the brand had grown to prominence for the purity of its product, which was distilled five times, a very costly procedure at the time. The vodka was such a resounding success that Smith, already affluent thanks to his many business ventures, quickly became one of the richest men in Stockholm, with massive estates and a luxurious apartment overlooking the city's royal castle. But it was not only with business that Smith occupied his attention. He strove to better workers' conditions by founding banks and cooperatives where they could buy better food at lower prices. He got himself elected to parliament and lobbied for legislation that would allow workers to vote. His renegade ways ultimately got him into trouble, and after a dire illness from which he unexpectedly survived, he lost most of his fortune. Not to be out dealt by fate, he quickly rebuilt his wealth, before, in later life, retiring to relative modesty.

Certainly Patrick could not have overlooked the parallels with his own father's life.

Patrick Ricard at the 50th company birthday, 1982.

Chapter Nine

LIVING IN ISOLATION NEVER COULD HAVE SUITED PAUL. The idea of being perched on a mountain surrounded by wild terrain pleased him in theory. He took up residence in a small shepherd's shack with a chimney he had built himself. "I've been fighting for 40 years," he told his friends to justify his decision. "I've heard others talk about playing *pétanque*. I would like to play myself. And if it rains, to play a game of cards."

But it was not long before Paul's brain started ticking with new projects. He never fully cut the ties to his active ambition. His Mercedes 600 sedan was waiting with a chauffeur at the ready to take him to town or to the private airport just a short drive away if he needed to venture farther afield. Movement had defined his life. A sedentary existence would not suit his energetic disposition. Retirement could not mean inaction. His next saga would need to crown his prior achievements. Now he could go about his projects differently, for his own pleasure and to defend the principles that he believed in so strongly. He would no longer be working with the old parameters. He no longer had to worry about his firm. He could be more idealistic, more radical.

Already he had shown that he could rally in the name of a cause. In 1966 an environmental disaster threatened the marine life off the coast of Marseille when a new sewage pipe was installed, spewing refuse of "red mud" full of bauxite (mostly a by-product of the aluminum industry nearby) into the sea. Paul had loved the sea since his youth, when he believed his convalescence in Sausset-les-Pins had cured his illness. He decided something concrete needed to be done. He stoked staunch community support in opposition and also opened a marine observatory on the Ile des Embiez to study the level of pollution in the sea and its impact on marine biodiversity. Paul recruited the help of Alain Bombard, a scientist and sea adventurer, to his cause.

Bombard was just the type of renegade who attracted Paul's respect. Just like Paul, Bombard could not be told what to do. Trained

Paul Ricard Oceanographic Institute, built in 1966.

as a doctor, he had decided to study the impact on the human body of being stranded at sea. He wanted to prove that man could survive alone at sea well beyond what anyone expected if equipped with a proper life raft and nourishment. To prove his point, in 1952, he voluntarily shipwrecked himself by setting off in a rubber raft from the Canary Islands. Living essentially on rainwater and plankton, he arrived two-and-a-half months later in Barbados in the Caribbean. The transatlantic voyage had been grueling: he had lost almost 60 pounds and was emaciated, weak, and sickly. But he was alive. Over the entirety of his trip he had carefully noted the effects on his body, measuring his heartbeat, etc., and treating his transatlantic survival voyage as a serious scientific experience. Paul admired Bombard's tenacity and resistance in sticking to his task in the most trying of circumstances.

Paul's observatory was designed to examine all aspects of the ocean and how best to preserve the natural balance of its life. Over the years, the foundation grew in importance, organizing clean ocean days and spearheading vast programs of research to improve knowledge of the ocean and how to preserve its life, so vital to our own. An aquarium was opened in the 1970s that drew thousands of visitors a year, mostly with the aim of educating them to the delicate nature of marine life.

After his incredible resignation, projects such as this continued to circle in Paul's mind. The house at Tête de L'Evêque became an obsession all its own. He built it up into a genuine compound, far from the madding crowd. The wind whipped up the hill and through the scrub brush and the sun beat down in the hottest summer months, when Paul liked to escape by taking his boat on long trips in the Mediterranean. For a visitor to the place, the house did not appear to be the abode of a business mogul. It was a place for a man who wanted to be alone, for someone totally uninterested by the conventions of social life. Nothing was for show, so much so that a first-time visitor to the place could feel a little perplexed at the house's absence of grandeur. It was large, but monastic, the bedrooms cell-like, stripped of any apparent luxuries, with the main rooms geared toward work rather than relaxation. In fact, besides the dining room, with its bar and piano, there are few places in the house where one could imagine resting.

There was a distillery laboratory, where Paul spent his afternoons concocting new brews and testing old ones. These types of experiments represented the beginnings of his success, a fact he did not want to neglect. The library shelves were crammed with books, mostly historical in nature or dedicated to the study of a particular subject. Paul was keen on reading about the history of Provence, as he felt a responsibility to protect the region that was his home. In fact, he felt so strongly about his home that he even agreed to run for mayor of Signes, where his house was located. It is a small *commune*, or community, of some 1,000 people. But its size did not shield Paul from large headaches.

"If it hadn't been for building permits, I would have built more than Louis XIV," Paul liked to say.

He locked horns with the French national administration on many of the projects he tried to accomplish in Signes, including a scheme to

Paul Ricard waving on his boat the Garlaban, 1975.

secure the area from wild fires. When he wrote to the French president Georges Pompidou to present his plans and gain formal clearance and funding, he waited in vain for an answer, which he finally received months later from an anonymous ministry offering vague support but no particulars. For a man like Paul, whose whole existence had been about living in the moment and pushing through immediate results, the world of politics, with its drawn out negotiations and endless concessions, hardly suited his temperament. It was a miracle that he lasted eight years, from 1972 to 1980, in his role as mayor. He treated his role with much of the same flair that he had shown as president of Ricard. Small pamphlets of his mayoral speeches were printed and circulated to keep the community abreast of all news and projects.

Paul's distaste of administration continued even though he was now part of it. In 1976, he even threatened to quit his mayor's post, totally disgusted by official opposition to his projects.

In a discourse delivered in November 1976, Paul elaborated on his reasons for wanting to quit.

"The builder finds fulfillment in the happiness he gives to others," he said. "Unfortunately, we live in a country run by an unimaginative system, ignorant of the evolution of life. We are prisoners to rules that have become more and more complicated and whose origins date to the time where men walked or rode horses."

He continued, "My declarations aren't designed to make me friends. I won't have more enemies either. All that I will have done to hurt them is to have said the truth in public that they refuse to listen to.

"Things being as they are, faced with the negation and powerlessness of democracy and with much regret … it seems pointless to me that I remain your mayor."

Nonetheless, the community refused to accept his resignation and convinced Paul to continue for another four years before he finally threw in the towel.

Two years later, Paul reiterated his intention to quit as mayor, only again to be convinced to continue for an additional two years. Again, in one of his harangues against the state, he scolded the centralized French government: "The nation has become the servant of the state: a state that is sovereign and all powerful."

Paul was no politician and he had no stomach for the political process that constituted the backbone of the French government. Its raison d'être was anathema to his as an entrepreneur. He saw things pragmatically, locally, and topically. It was at best an uneasy position for him to endure.

Just as at Ricard, where his employees adulated him to such a degree that it sometimes bordered on hero worship, the townspeople of Signes had come to rely on Paul, with his unbridled energy and endless optimism, for improvement.

When Paul required time alone, he retreated to his house on the hill. His love of painting remained undimmed. He never understood abstract art. For him, art was meant to be comprehended and universal. If a painting needed to be decoded, dissected, explained, it wasn't true art in his eyes. It was just like the music that he listened to when he painted. It was harmonious, always classical. The value of that music was solid, Paul was sure. He was less convinced of the worth of pop music and modern atonal compositions. He thought they, too, like abstract art, would certainly fade away eventually. What people couldn't understand immediately did not appeal to Paul.

When he wanted to work with his hands in another manner, he retreated to the woodworking studio he had installed on the house's top level, replete with hammers, saws, block planes, and calipers. The smell of fresh-cut wood transported Paul into a peaceful zone. He spent hours drawing and creating to-scale models of boats. It was one of his great passions. Indeed, he had designed his own yacht, the *Garlaban*, which took its name from the 2,400-foot-high mountain overlooking Marseille. Over the years, he found numerous ways to improve the ship, including changing the situation of the cabins to increase comfort for all during his many prolonged sailing outings across the Mediterranean.

Paul's passion for boat building was such that he got involved

Paul Ricard explaining plans in his shipyard at Les Embiez, 1964 (left). Marie-Thérèse Ricard on the Garlaban, 1959.

with the financing of the construction of an advanced three-hulled trimaran sailing boat for the legendary French sailor Eric Tabarly. Named the *Paul Ricard*, the boat was designed with the idea of breaking the transatlantic speed record, held by Charlie Barr since 1905. Tabarly and his crew shattered the long-standing record in a legendary crossing in 1980 that took just over 10 days.

Paul had bought a large patch of land on the plateau between Marseille and Toulon long ago, with the intention of turning its rocky terrain into a village for his employees including tennis courts, pools, playgrounds for children, and houses. It had been one of Paul's most ambitious projects, capsized by an endless labyrinth of administrative red tape. Eventually, Paul canceled the project and, less ambitiously, he used some of the land to construct a small airport.

Paul always felt that his ideas for the land were only partially realized, and after his retirement from Ricard he decided to do something with it by building a world-class racing circuit.

Clearing the project with the sticky French building regulators and administration would not be easy. He knew that red tape would accumulate as soon as he announced his plans. To circumvent those problems he enlisted the help of the top Formula One racing drivers, including legends such as Jackie Stewart and Jacky Ickx. Paul wanted the track to be the safest and most advanced in the world.

Racing in the late 1960s and 1970s was a sport tainted by death. It was downright dangerous. Eight drivers died in the late 1960s and nine in the 1970s.

It didn't take long for the site to be transformed completely by

Paul Ricard on the circuit construction site, 1969.

a battalion of motor graders and tractors. Paul showed up in the mornings dressed in jeans, a blue anorak and a red cap. He drove a tractor himself and guided the work like a field general. When people showed up to visit, they found Paul working. As ever, he still enjoyed getting his hands dirty.

Outsourcing was something he did not know how to do. He accomplished every one of his projects by applying his brain to a problem and attempting to improve what already existed.

The track took form with incredible speed. Work whizzed on through the cold winter months of rain and terrible wind. Tons of earth were moved. The track's particularity would be more than one-mile-long straight stretch where drivers could achieve dizzying speed.

Paul was used to dealing with French administration and their stymieing his building plans. When he bought more than 170 acres on the Domaine de Roustagnon, near Bendor, with the intention of building housing for the Spanish workers he had recruited to work at the glassworks on the island, Paul had to climb through a labyrinth of regulations before he obtained the green light. Even after the project was completed, it drew unwanted attention from tax authorities, who threatened to put and end to the project by overtaxing the inhabitants Paul housed there on claims that their accommodation was cheaper than it should be compared to the rest of the national average. Paul never could stomach these administrative struggles. Certainly, he was used to them. He had so many projects on the go that the tango between him and the French administration went on for years. When Paul tried to build a center for his workers in Rennes, for instance, it was blackballed because its buildings were too traditional looking. When building another factory, the plans came under scrutiny because they were too modern for the administrative seal. Paul felt like these refusals and protracted waits had become personal. He had drawn up the plans for many of the projects himself, always with the well-being of his workers in mind. "If the Greeks had had the French building administration they would never have finished the Acropolis," he told a reporter once.

Paul no longer wanted to make concessions. He often thought back to his helicopter accident. Strangely, he remembered a dog that had started barking when he was taking off. Over his life, Paul had found significance in the most violent acts to shake his being. Was it the dog that caused a moment of lost concentration for Paul and thus the crash? Or was it the dog that was trying to tell him not to take off?

Such moments of reflection made him consider not only his achievements, their value, and impact, but also everything he continued to strive to achieve. Paul's view of life became more radical as he grew older for the simple reason that he knew he had no time to waste. Airs and graces had never been his style. Paul never worked for riches in and of themselves. He lived well, but as he grew older the trappings of wealth, some of which he had used earlier to levy prestige for his company, held even less value to him. He did not live in a palace. To his children and their children after them he wanted to impart a philosophy of work and honesty. Success, Paul believed, came from the application of one's talents to a cause. It should never come free. It should never come easy.

He built his legend at the same time and in the same way that he constructed his firm, leaving little to chance and telling his story through books, films, and multiple taped interviews. His story was so well constructed that talking to one of his friends or family members often yields little deviation from what one or the other relates.

Not every one was his friend, a fact that mattered little to Paul. His tastes were his own. He liked the sea, nature, solid old homes, and mostly straightforward art. He was happier eating a bit of sausage and cheese with a glass of his pastis than a fancy five-star spread. Likewise, he would rather spend an afternoon in the company of working men than with so-called sophisticates pontificating about rarified ideals. Paul Ricard knew himself, and that was probably one of the greatest reasons that success came to him with the facility it did. He never strove to be or to achieve something beyond his character. He was what he was.

It is without a doubt one of the reasons he wanted to be buried on Les Embiez Island after his death on November 7, 1997 at 88 years of age. His grave is a simple stone, jagged by nature but polished by the inexorable wind that whips from the sea. It is perched on a small cliff, high above the shore with a remarkable vista across the blue Mediterranean. Nothing is fancy, but it is solid and the surroundings are majestic. Paul would have been both happy and sad to know that his second son, Patrick, who died of a violent heart attack in 2012, joined him in his idyllic resting place.

Paul had imparted to Patrick a philosophy of life that his son

Paul Ricard and his son Patrick are buried on Les Embiez Island.

took as his own but then molded to his own vision. While Paul had created, Patrick had expanded, making Pernod Ricard into one of the world's top multinational drinks groups through a program of aggressive acquisitions.

Yet one of the most endearing achievements of the two men is the creation not only of a firm, but of a culture. Paul's ideas of work, his dreams rooted in Provence, and his way of being with others permeate his company to this day. Company culture is not only results and sales, it is the force that drives those sales today and tomorrow.

When the company and its employees meet for yearly powwows on Les Embiez Island, this spirit comes out. Conviviality rules and the men and women who work at Pernod Ricard, although many may not know the details of Paul's life, feel the force of the ideas he instilled throughout his firm.

It is a testimony to the strength of the man.

In a more private ceremony, the members of the Ricard clan, as many as four generations of them, meet together before such company congregations. They climb the hill on the island where Paul and Patrick's bodies lie. Glasses are distributed and filled with pastis, water and ice. The glasses are raised as the family members break into song.

The song they sing is the hymnal of Ricard.

Ô toi, Sainte-Marthe
Reine du Pataclet
Sers avant qu'on ne parte
Un bon Ricard bien frais!
Ave, ave, ave cinq volumes d'eau (Bis)...

Paul Ricard in 1964, leaving his private aerodrome at home in Le Castelet.

PAUL RICARD

Epilogue

vers la fin de mes jours en ce début d'année je ne peux que vous dire n'oubliez jamais la devise qui grave dans la pierre de cette île de Bendor

Nul bien sans peine.

et le riche laboureur qui fut sage de m'instruire avant sa mort a ses enfants que le travail est un trésor !

"In this New Year, toward the end of my days, I can only ask that you never forget the motto that's engraved in stone on this island of Bendor:

No pain, no gain

And the rich farmer, who had been wise to show his children before his death that work is a treasure!"

-Paul Ricard

THE FARMER AND HIS CHILDREN

Work hard, sweat all you can:
Riches is what counts the least.
A rich farmer, feeling his impending death,
Sent for his children, and talked to them without witnesses.
Do not sell the inheritance left by our parents, he said,
As a treasure is hidden in it.
I don't know the spot, but with a bit of courage
You will find it, you will figure it out.
Go search the field when summer ends.
Dig, plow, leave no earth unturned
Anywhere your hands can reach.
After the father's death, the sons worked the field
Everywhere, over and over again, so that within a year
It produced more than ever before.
There was no money to be found, but the father had been wise
To show them before his death
That work is a treasure.

Jean de la Fontaine